Seasons of Grace

Reflections on
the Orthodox Church Year

by DONNA FARLEY

CONCILIAR PRESS
Ben Lomond, California

SEASONS OF GRACE:
Reflections on the Orthodox Church Year
© Copyright 2002 by Donna Farley

Published by   Conciliar Press
                    P.O. Box 76
                    Ben Lomond, California 95005-0076

Printed in the United States of America

ISBN 1-888212-50-0

Contents

Part III:
God Incarnate

Part IV:
Open to Me the Gates of Repentance

Part V:
Lent, The Great Fast

Table of Contents

Many thanks are due for this present volume:

- to the various editors of *The Handmaiden* and Conciliar Press who made possible first the column and now the book—Katherine Hyde, Ginny Nieuwsma, Mary Armstrong, Carla Zell, and Father Thomas Zell

- to my husband, Fr. Lawrence Farley, for being my in-house expert on scriptural and liturgical references

- to fellow writers and friends who read various chapters and offered help—Bev M. Cooke, Linda and Sandy Finlayson

- to His Grace Bishop Seraphim for help with "Season's Greetings"

- to Marty Helgesen for introducing me to "Rose Is Rose"

There are doubtless others I have forgotten whom God will remember.

Introduction

The View from the Tightrope

I AM A CALENDAR ADDICT. I love that orderly progression of numbers, I guess, and the sense of seeing into the future as I turn the pages. Of course, you might just call the former a symptom of neurosis, and the latter a sign of an overactive imagination. But all human cultures share this ancient impulse to mark time. As a people develops their history, they establish their calendar as a way of observing past events, in hopes of predicting the future.

This begins with the agricultural year. The measurement of days and moons and seasons, with recurrent patterns of precipitation and temperature levels, helps the farmer choose the best times to plant and harvest. But as a nation goes through its birth pangs, it places an additional layer on top of the natural year. Thus, for instance, the Passover becomes a central focus in the round of Israel's calendar. The Torah prescribes a regular succession of sacrifices and festivals marking such events as the new moon or harvest; but throughout the history of Israel, added to these observances of natural seasons we have the celebration of historical events such as God's liberation of the children of Israel from Egypt (Passover) or Esther's triumph (Purim). Such holidays have both a ritual and a social character in many cultures, being occasions for the gathering of family and community to make religious observances such as prayer and sacrifice, and to reunite with seldom-seen friends and relatives for festal meals and other activities.

Modern secular nations too celebrate their history in a variety of community-binding holidays based on datable events. They sing patriotic songs, put on military displays, and have family get-togethers with food, food, food.

The Christian Church over the ages has developed its own round of feasts and seasons, distinct from either those of ancient Israel or the secular national calendars of the nations of the Christian era, though it has roots in both. After the peace of the Church under Constantine (A.D. 313), the Church calendar, in both Eastern and Western versions, became the dominant matrix for life in Christian countries.

In the twenty-first century, however, we are living in a clearly post-Christian world, and new time-marking procedures reflect that fact. Where once we marked all history as dating from the Year of Our Lord (A.D., *Anno Domini*) or B.C. (Before Christ), secular agencies are now pushing for the usage B.C.E., "Before Common Era," or C.E., "Common Era." Where Sunday in the Western world was once sacred and untouchable, few now complete their working lives without being required by employers to labor at least occasionally on that day, not only for essential services like hospitals and police work, but even for commercial endeavors—especially, in fact, in the retail and service industries that provide the majority of entry-level jobs for young people. Where Christmas was once a celebration of God With Us, we now find unbridled consumerism on one hand, and generic Midwinter Festivities on the other.

To be a Christian in this post-Christian world offers many challenges, just as it did in the first centuries A.D. In those days, a catechumenate of up to three years was required before the candidate was baptized into the fellowship. This lengthy period not only allowed for thorough theological instruction and a testing of the seriousness of commitment, it also sent the candidate on a journey through the seasons of the Church year, more than once.

Modern converts to the Eastern Orthodox Church, regardless of the length of their catechumenal period, know how bewildering a first tour through the now highly developed liturgical year can be. The depth and complexity of the festal cycle may at first be overwhelming to individuals raised in today's secular culture of short attention spans, or with the stripped-down worship of choruses–sermon–altar call prevalent in non-liturgical churches. But a second year of the revolving seasons brings the neophyte many *aha!* moments, excited responses to recognized themes and music, new insights into things not quite grasped the first time around.

For the so-called cradle Orthodox, and for the maturing convert of many years, each new repetition of Pascha or Christmas evokes memories of previous feasts, as well as pointing to the spiritual world that lies beyond the borders of this earthly space and time. Every feast is enriched not only by all those feasts that came before it, but also by our own new experiences on our life's pilgrimage. One never looks upon the Feast of the Dormition of the Theotokos in quite the same way again after having lost a loved one. Christmas is a new feast altogether when there is a first grandchild in the family fold. Pascha shines brighter than ever when we have the joy of sponsoring an adult godchild at his chrismation on Holy Saturday.

Whatever our background, Orthodox Christians in the modern world face a complexity of life that neither the ancient Israelites nor the Christians in the days of the state churches ever had to bear. Our entire society does not shut down for the Sabbath, or for Pascha. National feasts, with attendant family holiday pressures, sometimes clash with the fasting periods prescribed by the Church. In our everyday lives, we meet with a hundred instances of peer pressure, family demands, popular culture, and mushrooming technology, all seeming to have nothing to do with the stately progression of the Twelve Great Feasts re-enacting the story of God Incarnate.

When I began writing my column "Seasons of Grace" for *The Handmaiden*, it was this tension between the Church Year and the pressures of our society that intrigued me. We sometimes find ourselves walking a tightrope between what we think is the ideal of a holy life and the demands of our post-modern world; and it is all too easy to fall off on one side or the other. On the one side we may become isolationist, fearful, and legalistic, while on the other we may give up the struggle, go with the current of the world as it pulls us into complacency, pleasure-seeking, and materialism.

The beauty of the Church seasons is that they teach us how to balance our life. The succession of feast and fast tells us that God does not demand either too much of us, or too little. The Christian life is a whole life, an expansive life, a life in Christ, who gives Himself for the life of the world. The calendar of the Church is not meant to be experienced in isolation from the marketplace any more than the Church is meant to be insular or self-enclosed. We exist to serve Christ's pleasure—which is to bring Him to the world and the world to Him.

The present volume therefore is not a primer of the origins of the feasts and fasts, or of their liturgical services; there are several excellent volumes already to serve those purposes. This is, rather, a collection of my own reflections on the view from the tightrope. It seems to me that every year we repeat the cycle, the tightrope is raised a notch higher. When we look at something from a higher vantage point, we can see more than we did before. As we look at the world and the Church from these heights, what becomes apparent is not only the differences but the similarities. For Orthodoxy does not view the world as evil, but only as fallen, in need of and in waiting for the redemption Christ offers.

God's creation is good; and we humans, bent and broken though we may be, are the crown of that creation, the beings made in His own Image. It is no surprise to Orthodoxy, therefore, that humans are born with that impulse to create, in imitation of the One who created us. That God-breathed impulse is not negated even in this fallen world, and that is why, when I check the view from the tightrope, I spot angels appearing in both icons and syndicated comic strips; discern spiritual significance in homemade soup; and find Indiana Jones rubbing elbows with St. Ephraim the Syrian.

The reflections in this book are my own idiosyncratic ones, born out of a particular life in a certain time and place. I hope it will bless you to share in them; but more importantly, I hope they will encourage you to study the view from your own tightrope-walk. It may seem a little scary at first to look down from the heights, but if we simply keep on putting one foot in front of the other on our walk through the Church Year, we will surely arrive safely—by grace.

Part I

Beginning the Year

September 1
Church New Year

Back to School

WHEN WAS THE LAST TIME you began something new? At the beginning of college, perhaps, or a new job? When you got married or had a child or moved to a new town? Maybe one of the most significant new beginnings you recall now was your conversion to the Orthodox Faith, or joining a new parish.

Or it could be the most recent time you started something new was today. Maybe you started a book you'd never read before, or tried a new recipe, or met a new coworker. Newness is everywhere in God's world, if we look for it—echoes and foreshadowings of the new life in Christ that we are promised in baptism.

Each year at the beginning of September we have another chance to experience this newness on the first day of the liturgical year. The long and complex history of the Church's interaction with various states throughout Western civilization has resulted in a specially blessed coincidence for us Orthodox in North America: our Church year begins at about the same time as the academic year. At the same time as many members of the Church or their children are preparing to begin a new level in their education, the Church welcomes all of us to a "course of studies." This is why we are called "disciples." A disciple is a learner, a student. But not one who reads through the Bible in a higgledy-piggledy manner—one who, rather, follows a *discipline*. We have such a discipline in the Church's liturgical cycle, a complete and orderly celebration of the history of God's

15

dealings with His people. In fact, unlike in elementary school, high school, or university, we are studying one subject only: God. And there is no graduation until the end of this life. Learning is not a preparation for life, it *is* life. For in our school—the Church in all her aspects, whether liturgical services, Sunday school or Bible study, service to the needy, or fellowship with other members—we not only learn *about* God, we learn to know Him and to follow Him.

Do you remember getting ready for the first day of school when you were a child? The anticipation of reunion with old classmates . . . the last-minute checks to be sure you had every last pencil in your bag, every fold of new clothes (a size too big) in place . . . the butter-flies in the stomach?

The butterflies were there because of the newness. Part fear, part curiosity, part a kind of thrill that we were about to take our place with "the big kids," that we had grown since last year and belonged in the next grade now, even if the new clothes did still hang a little loosely.

What preparations do we make as we embark on this new year in the Church? How about a little "back-to-school shopping"? As children, and older students as well, are caught up in the hustle and bustle of gathering supplies and trying on fashionable new outfits, and working people come back from vacation with perhaps a sigh at returning to the old grind, wouldn't this be a good time to think about acquiring some things to aid you in your spiritual studies?

Have you set aside an icon corner? Do you have a saint's icon for each member of the family? Do you have a copy of the *Orthodox Study Bible, The Year of Grace of the Lord* by A Monk of the Eastern Church, or other spiritual reading? Do you keep a prayer rope at your bedside, or a little notebook for names of people to pray for in your icon corner? Your priest can advise you on many such matters, and help you find out where to get these things.

Who can forget that traditional first essay of the new school year, "What I did on my summer vacation"? The new Church year is a time for review, too—taking stock, remembering with thank-fulness, then preparing for the new routine. Some people may find it useful to make their "New Year's resolutions" now, rather than in

January. And this is an excellent time to plan on coming to confession.

One last aspect of going "back to school" is important to remember: the encouragement of "school spirit" in the gathering of community. Many parishes like to hold their Sunday school picnic or other social event to bring everyone together at this time of year. Some who practice general confession may find this a good time for it, or for a Saturday retreat to focus on the challenges to come. Others make a point of acknowledging the return of students to school (and particularly the students and teachers of the parish Sunday school) with a special prayer after the Liturgy.

The bell will ring early this September, on Sunday morning, with "Blessed is the Kingdom!" Don't be late!

September 8
Nativity of the Theotokos

The Beginning of the Beginning

"ONCE THERE WERE FOUR CHILDREN whose names were Peter, Susan, Edmund and Lucy. This story is about something that happened to them when they were sent away from London during the war...."

So begins one of the greatest of children's classics, *The Lion, the Witch, and the Wardrobe,* by C. S. Lewis. But this isn't the real beginning of the story. It began much earlier, in the thoughts of its author. And in his dreams.

Lewis complained that no-one else seemed to be writing the kind of stories that he wished to read; therefore he resolved to write one himself. Amid his unfruitful attempts to produce a children's fairy story about a magical world, he began to have dreams about lions. And so it was that Aslan was born into Narnia, to roar the roar of love that has captivated readers young and old for more than half a century.

The lion dream was the *beginning* of the beginning of the Narnia series. There is a similar "beginning of the beginning" to the Church year.

The Orthodox Church calendar is a strange beast, comprising parts drawn from different sources at different times. Like the mythical gryphon—half eagle, half lion—it may strike us as unnatural, and yet, somehow, it flies. It begins in historical time, with September 1, the Byzantine New Year's Day; and the dates of saints' deaths, the translation of their relics, the occurrence of miraculous events, or other such celebrations are reckoned according to this Byzantine chronology.

Just a week after this Byzantine civil New Year's Day, we have on September 8 what we might call the Beginning of the Beginning of the festal cycle within the calendar year—the first of the Twelve Great Feasts, the Nativity of the Theotokos.

When I was an evangelical, I never knew there were such things as church feasts. We celebrated Christmas with a carol service and Easter with a couple of Resurrection-themed hymns. When I became a member of a Western liturgical church, I discovered the thrill of Christmas anticipation with the lighting of candles in an Advent wreath for four Sundays before the twenty-fifth.

But Orthodoxy, as you know, is never content with half-measures! Our Church calendar goes back *beyond* the beginning of the Incarnational story, beyond the Nativity of Our Lord and God and Savior Jesus Christ, to the Nativity of His Mother, celebrated on September 8.

If we listen to the lessons and hymnography of this feast, of course, we discover that even here, at the Beginning of the Beginning, we have not yet reached the true depths of the genesis of the story. Indeed what appears on the surface to be the "beginning of the beginning" is really only a place of transition.

The Old Testament lessons and hymns for the day speak of Mary the Virgin Theotokos (literally "Birth-giver" or Mother of God) as "the Gate," "the Ladder," or "the Bridge." The *Proto-evangelion of James*, second-century A.D. source for much of this festal material, even sets the city gate as the meeting place of the joyful Joachim and Anna, when they hasten from their separate angelic visions to share the good news that their barrenness is ended, that they are to have a child whose name will become illustrious throughout all the world. An old story is ending; a new one is beginning.

In my workshops for Christian writers, I lead the students to explore what has to happen *before* the beginning begins. "Sing, Heavenly Muse!" cries John Milton, invoking the Holy Spirit to inspire him to tell the tale of *Paradise Lost*. The dream of lions did not come to Lewis by accident or without preparation. It came because of who he was and what he did. A classical scholar and atheist-turned-Christian, he was certainly familiar with the *Physiologus*, a third-century work that drew morals from the habits and character of animals, including a comparison of the lion with Christ, the Lion of Judah.

Like Joachim and Anna, writers repeatedly experience barrenness. As with those who long for children, all the desire, all the medical remedies in the world are not enough; even some agnostic writers will admit there is a certain something beyond their ability to effect, the inspiration of the muse. Not all writers pray like Milton to the Heavenly Muse, but all wait for this inspiration. There is a very important key, though, that distinguishes the professional writer from the amateur. Both writers wait for inspiration—but the professional does not wait idly. He reads, studies, thinks, practices. By who they are and what they do, writers prepare to be the bridge, the gate by which a story can be born into the world and reach readers.

I think that is the purpose of the Feast of the Nativity of the Theotokos for us. As we anticipate the Beginning, we are not to wait idly, but to seek to allow God to prepare us for His use. Like Milton and Lewis with their stories, the Theotokos was prepared for her role as a Bridge and a Gate by her life, from birth and even before, by God's working in her parents' lives. And she is the model of all Christians.

Saint Seraphim of Sarov is one who patterned himself faithfully after that model, as reflected in his famous phrase, "Acquire the Spirit of peace, and thousands around you will be saved." At the beginning of the beginning of the Twelve Feasts, we come to seek inspiration, to seek Christ. God does not need our worship; our hymns and processions, however beautiful, do not compare in the least to the heavenly adoration of the cherubim and seraphim. It is we who need this incarnational story cycle, the celebration of God's mighty works in Christ. The Church year too is a gate, bringing Christ to birth within us, so that we in turn may be, like the Theotokos and Saint Seraphim, a bridge between Christ and the world.

September 14
Exaltation of the Cross

Holy Archeology

WHEN I WAS IN ABOUT GRADE 7, I wanted to be an archeologist. This was well before Indiana Jones's big-screen adventures, mind you, and the luminous names that caught my fancy were those of real people, like Heinrich Schliemann, who excavated the ruins of Troy. What all the world had thought no more than a myth he triumphantly brought to light—confirmation of an epic story, and undreamt-of treasure.

Archeology has its own patron saint—St. Helena, the mother of the Emperor Constantine. As a result of the medieval trafficking in relics, the mere idea of holy archeology was subsequently pooh-poohed by the Reformation and (so-called) Enlightenment. But although we have little reliable historical evidence for it, St. Helena's story is not necessarily such a stretch, when you stand it beside Schliemann's. Troy fell and was buried, but the Cross, according to Holy Tradition, was deliberately concealed by the faithful, who feared its destruction by the invaders of Jerusalem.

The Feast of the Elevation of the Cross commemorates the date in A.D. 335 upon which the Church of the Holy Sepulchre, where a relic believed to be a remnant of the Cross was kept, was dedicated in Jerusalem; the date was later made a celebration of the Cross in Constantinople. Because the Holy Cross is of such central importance to the Church, this Feast Day is now numbered with the rest of the Twelve Great Feasts dedicated to Christ and His Mother.

"The light of Your countenance has been signed on us," runs the verse (taken from the Septuagint rendering of Psalm 4:6, 7) used at communion for the Feast of the Cross. It calls to mind the tracing of the cross upon our foreheads, hearts, hands, and feet with Holy Chrism when we are received into the Orthodox Church, whether as infants or as adult converts.

Invisibly the Holy Spirit embeds this same sign in our hearts. But then, so often, something happens. By carelessness or idolatry, the Cross is buried in our lives. "Deny yourself, take up your cross and follow Me, or you cannot be My disciple," says Our Lord. But how do we take it up when we cannot find it? How do we take it up when we have forgotten all about it?

I once heard a Protestant evangelical complain that Orthodoxy did not concentrate on the cross enough. I can't imagine what made him think this. And yet it is rather easy for us to forget it, perhaps because we are in fact *too* used to seeing it and hearing about it all around us, all the time. We don't have to dig for it in church—if we are present at services, or even in the building at all, it's "in our face." If it is hidden, it is hidden in plain sight. The Cross stands triumphantly atop the church dome; it decorates doors, woodwork within the church, clerical vestments, liturgical vessels. The cross hangs about our necks, next to our skin, from the time of our baptism; we trace it upon ourselves in prayer, sing of it repeatedly.

We dedicate three major feasts to the Cross in the year, and commemorate it every Wednesday and Friday as well. We bear it as a triumphal standard at the head of processions, adorn it with floral offerings, and prostrate ourselves before it in veneration and awe.

But away from a liturgical setting, as the everyday rubble of hurry and worry comes crashing down over our lives, perhaps we do need to excavate a bit to find the cross and expose its shining summons to the world, and to ourselves. Before Jesus said, "Take up your cross," He said "Deny yourself." He knew that was what it would mean for us to follow Him. Noone picks up a cross and carries it for the fun of it; if you are carrying your cross it means that, like Jesus, you are on the road to your death.

When we consider the cross on Wednesdays and Fridays, it rather puts into perspective the small ascetic feats prescribed for us by the church on those days. How can we care about not getting to put cream in our coffee, on a day when we recall how Christ loved us to the point of offering up Himself as a sacrifice for our sins? For this reason it is appropriate that September 14 alone of the Twelve Great Feasts is a strict fast day, in keeping with the immensity and solemnity of the commemoration.

How can we uncover the cross that lies buried in our hearts? By the self-denial of the Church's fasts; by the death to self that comes through self-examination and confession. The Feast of the Elevation of the Cross, a penitential fasting-feast, situated so near the beginning of the Church year, is an ideal time for confession, spiritual direction, and the preparation of spiritual goals and discipline.

Archeology is heavy, dirty, physical work, and requires persistence and meticulous patience. (I think I know why I never became an archeologist after all!) But when at last he hauls the buried treasure up into the air of the present, the archeologist knows that all the sweat and privation and frustrating false starts have been worth it. Photographs are published in the *National Geographic*, and soon the whole world is sharing his excitement.

So it is for us. We need to uncover the sign of the cross in our hearts, and raise it up as the icons show St. Helena doing. In the words of an old favorite Western hymn, "Lift high the Cross, the Love of Christ proclaim / Till all the world adore His sacred Name."

Part II

Prepare Ye the Way

November 8
St. Michael and the Heavenly Bodiless Powers

The Beauty and the Terror of Angels

"Supreme leaders of the Heavenly Hosts, we implore you ceaselessly to encircle us, unworthy as we are, with the shelter of your prayers, and to cover us beneath the wings of your immaterial glory. We fall down before you crying aloud, protect us from all dangers, O Princes of the Powers on High."

—Troparion to the Archangels

"LET'S HAVE AN ANGEL PARTY!"

Advent was coming, you see. Our choir wanted to kick up their heels one last time before the fast—and what could be more appropriate than to celebrate the choir's patrons, those most accomplished of singers, the Heavenly Bodiless Powers, whose feast falls on November 8, just a week before Advent itself begins?

We strung twinkling white lights about the living room and raided my daughters' collections of Christmas ornaments. Every year on St. Nicholas Day (December 6), new ornaments appear in the shoes left outside their bedroom doors—and nearly all of these ornaments, as it happens, are in the form of angels. Now like the herald angels in the Christmas story, these angel ornaments appeared in a cloud about the party room, proclaiming the coming celebration of Christ's Nativity. White and gold, crystal and ceramic, they caught and reflected the light, filling all with beauty.

In the Middle Ages there was a coin called an "angel," and like that coin, the heavenly angels have two sides. We, however, are accustomed only to the beautiful side. In recent years, angels have overflowed the boundaries of Christmas celebration to decorate the margins of New Age books, fill the knick-knack shelves at card shops, and even to grace television dramas.

These popular images of angels, like our ornaments, are delicate, aesthetically pleasing, sometimes homely and comforting, or even cute and sentimental. But in the Scriptures and liturgical texts, we frequently find the other side of angels—the side that makes mere mortals cower in terror when they encounter these pure beings. More often than not, the first words an angel is forced to speak to a mortal are "Fear not," for their radiant appearance is too overwhelming for us who are creatures of dust.

This other side of the angels is cleverly portrayed in Pat Brady's syndicated comic strip, *Rose Is Rose*. Rose's little boy Pasquale, with his innocent eyes, frequently sees and converses with his own guardian angel. Most of the time this angel looks just like Pasquale himself with wings, a halo, and a white robe. But occasionally his guardian duties require him to uncloak his warrior form, and he looms over the landscape, brandishing a huge sword, eyes burning, and with shoulders like Schwarzenegger.

At first glance, the angels on our Orthodox iconostasis may look more like Christmas ornaments than like Pasquale's fierce and mighty guardian angel. The angelic expressions are serene, their robes flowing, and their sexless features may appear effeminate next to the bearded saints who share the iconostasis with them. But the liturgical context is all in Orthodox worship, and for these icons of angels as for other elements, the full meaning cannot appear in isolation.

"Fiery is your appearance and miraculous is your beauty, O Michael the Archangel . . . by your might you are known as all-powerful. . . . *[O Lord]* . . . *Make your angels spirits as it is written, and your ministers a flaming fire* . . . first in boldness among the heavenly ones, standing in glory before the terrible throne, witness of inexpressible things . . . you O leader of hosts . . . glow with the unapproachable light of the glory of the Lord . . ."

The Vigil service for the eve of the feast honoring St. Michael and the other heavenly powers, drawing on scriptural texts, speaks repeatedly of them as champions and commanders of armies, and begs protection under the shadow of their wings. The radiance that emanates from these heavenly beings is *both* beautiful and terrible, for it is the fiery illumination of God Himself, the Holy Trinity.

No wonder, then, that the prayer appointed to be said to one's guardian angel begins as a trembling prayer for forgiveness for the offenses our sinful nature must give daily to creatures of such purity, and then asks for the protection their might can give us against the evil temptations that surround us.

When we think of these texts, the iconic angels are transformed before our eyes, and we notice that the formality of the Orthodox composition speaks of strength united with beauty; whereas more naturalistic Western art is mostly limited to one or the other at a time. Look sometime at an icon of a child's guardian angel. The child carries a scroll reading, "Take me by my wretched and outstretched hand." And the angel does hold the child's hand; while the angel is a graceful and serene figure, you can see the strength of the grip—you know he isn't going to let go!

Note too the weapons often carried by the angels who grace the iconostasis and walls of your parish church. Sometimes they carry a staff or standard, but sometimes it is a spear they hold. This spear, like the hands and facial features of all icons, is attenuated, to represent its spiritual quality, but it is a spear nevertheless, representative of the angel's power to strike against evil. St. Michael in particular is sometimes shown with a sword and armor, as he is the commander-in-chief of the heavenly armies, depicted in the Apocalypse as leading the charge against Satan and his hosts (Revelation 12:7).

Humans who see angels, the Scriptures tell us, most often react with terror (e.g., Daniel 10:5–12). The good news is that the angels tell us to "fear not"—but the fallen angels, the devil and his hosts, are still terrified of the mighty angelic guardians God has appointed for His people.

Perhaps angels are not like two-sided coins after all, but the radiance of their holy beauty itself is what terrifies. Perhaps it is only as we regain our own wholeness, the image of God being restored in us, that we can see the true image of the angels and of all of God's creation, not diffracted as in a prism, but unified in holy beauty and strength.

November 15
Beginning of Advent

Gifts of Time

ADVENT MEANS MANY THINGS: the scent of lentil soup in the kitchen, a sense of joyful anticipation in prayer times, the challenge to Orthodox asceticism of endless (pre-)Christmas parties with acquaintances and coworkers.

And it means shopping for Christmas gifts.

You've doubtless been told since you were a child that "it is more blessed to give than to receive" and "Christmas is more about giving than getting." This is only a beginning, however, to understanding what Christmas gifts are all about. Christmas giving needs to go beyond the polite reciprocity of the office gift pool, and even beyond the innocent joy of children finding that longed-for toy beneath the tree. To the worshipful heart, Christmas giving is, like all of life, sacramental, a means of entering into the life of the age to come.

The Christmas *litya* and *aposticha* verses (in the Vespers service) tell us that the wise men "hurried to Bethlehem. They offered Thee acceptable gifts. . . . Purest gold, for the King of the ages; frankincense, for the God of all; myrrh, for the immortal One, as though He were dead three days."

As so often in the hymns of the Church, these verses serve up paradoxical truth. What need for gold has a King who says plainly, "My kingdom is not of this world" (John 18:36)? The God who scorned Israel's burnt offerings ("If I were hungry, I would not tell you," Psalm 50:12) desires no frankincense. And while the verse marvels at myrrh (used to embalm the dead) as a gift for the Immortal One, at the same time it foreshadows the paradoxical death He will in fact submit to.

What then made these gifts "acceptable"? It would be facile to say only that the magi gave them from the heart. Orthodoxy imputes no validity to sentiment in itself. But look how they gave. They did not ring a bell for some servant and have him pop the parcels in the mailbox, nor even hire armed couriers to deliver the costly presents. They themselves *hurried* to Bethlehem. And however they made haste, they traveled with patience, for it was a long journey, perhaps as long as two years. And therein, I think, is the proof that in the hearts of the wise men was more than sentiment about a newborn child, more than excitement at knowing about a world-changing event. The frankincense, gold, and myrrh were all very well, and their symbolism re-echoes yet for us, but the magi gave much more, just to see the newborn King. They gave many months of their lives to an uncertain pilgrimage. They gave time.

In Advent it is precisely time that seems in such short supply as we struggle desperately to make a quiet space amid the social and commercial bustle of the world's selling season. The world does not understand time or its value. The children of this world do not wish to give their time to undertake the arduous Advent pilgrimage to the Nativity; instead, they begin to celebrate they know not what, long before the event and often in unholy manner. "Time is money," says the business adage. But time is very much more. Time applied to work may win us money, but there is no amount of money in the world that can buy back a squandered day, a wasted minute.

Thus consider the gifts we plan to give this Christmas. Indeed, we must devote time to planning the giving if they are not to be worldly gifts. If a child only wishes out loud for a particular toy, and it then appears under the tree, the parent may not have given enough time to thinking of a good gift. Is it a gift that will enrich the child's life by encouraging sharing—something like a soccer ball, whereby he or she will spend time with parents, siblings, or friends? Something that will develop the mind and soul, like a good book or educational toy? Or is it only the latest fad, something that in the week after Christmas will be revealed to be poorly made or will fail to hold the child's interest?

Families who learn to take time know the value of homemade gifts far exceeds that of the store-bought kind. Our children are in the habit of making us a videotape of a performance of their own devising each Christmas—and as I write this, in the first week of September, they are already taking the time to work on this year's entry. Other families with arts and crafts abilities are haunting the craft stores now, too, looking for the makings of wreaths, sweaters, plaster ornaments, and a thousand other items that will take shape as the days of autumn progress toward Bethlehem.

St. Nicholas as the gift-giver has become closely associated with the Christmas season in the West. My children and I bake cookies, to be distributed secretly on his feast, December 6. But how much less it would mean to both givers and recipients if we did not take the time to make our own cookies and instead stuffed the little bags with the products of Mr. Christie or Nabisco.

So often I find myself saying things like, "If I have time, I'll . . ." or "I wish I had time to . . ." But we do have time. God has given it to us—it was in fact the first of His gifts to His Creation, the morning and the evening and the days, even before He created life itself. Now we have the privilege of giving it back—"Thine own of Thine own we offer unto Thee," as the priest says of the eucharistic offering—by giving it today to the pilgrimage to Nativity.

This Advent, I wish you Godspeed, a Star to guide you, and that all your precious gifts may be acceptable as those of the magi.

November 15–December 24
The Advent Fast

Season's Greetings

HOW BLAND AND GENERIC are those words, "Season's Greetings." They appear on cards adorned with holly or poinsettias, and no Christian could fail to identify them with Christmas. Yet they carefully do not mention Christ or His Nativity. Such greeting cards are employed by businesses to spread to their customers the goodwill of a season we all know as none other than Christmas, but without risking the political incorrectness of the Holy Name.

In the world, "'tis the season," beginning in November or even October: the only season, the season for red-and-green decorations and selling and partying and sending those greeting cards (themselves a commercial invention first employed in the nineteenth century). For us Orthodox, though, there are many seasons, and there need be nothing so nondescript as "Season's Greetings" on our Christmas cards. Instead we use the joyous liturgical cry and its response, "Christ is Born!" "Glorify Him!"

In fact, the Church maintains a tradition of greetings peculiar to each season or occasion, not just Christmas.

Throughout the world's history, greetings have served numerous purposes, according to the context of their time and place. "*Pax vobiscum*" and "*Shalom*" or "*Salaam*" are examples of what is perhaps the most common of all greetings, "Peace," which from time immemorial has guarded encounters between people from the very real possibility of violence. It is both a declaration of the intent of peaceful behavior during the encounter, and an expressed wish that the other person and his household may have peace and prosperity.

Our liturgical greeting to one another in church, before the reception of communion, is also "Peace," following the salutation of the Apostles in their epistles to the faithful. But it is transformed from the world's assurance of a "cease-fire," for the prescribed greeting is more than simply "Peace." First the priest says, "Peace be with you!" and we respond, "And also with you." Then clergy at the altar embrace and exchange two or three kisses, according to their particular ethnic tradition, saying, "Christ is in our midst!" "He is and ever shall be!" because it is only with Christ in our midst that there can be true peace.

This exchange is performed increasingly among the laity as well. Though this may be controversial, and arguably subject to the abuse of devolving into a neighborly "hugfest," it can be practiced reverently. The Copts still preserve this older custom of the entire congregation participating in the greeting of the Peace: they make a graceful "salaam" by briefly taking their neighbors' folded palms between their own.

The "Orthodoxizing" of greeting may make the leap from the nave of the church to the parish hall by employing a beautiful Russian monastic custom. After grace, instead of a secular table greeting like "*Bon appetit!*" we may recall the hospitality of Abraham with the declaration, "The angel is at the table!"

The particular form of a greeting may establish the terms of relationship between the participants. We see in the Old Testament, for instance, prostrations being made to an elder, to a social superior, or to someone who is receiving an apology. In Japan, the depth of a bow conveys many nuances of how the two people meeting regard each other. Not long ago in North America, a man would briefly "tip his hat" in respect when greeting a woman.

Our own radically egalitarian culture employs such niceties of greeting only in the most limited manner. A salesman on a cold call might say, "Good morning, sir," or "Good afternoon, ma'am," but the more usual greeting, even among those only casually acquainted, is something more like, "Hi, howya doin'?" "Fine, thanks," is the response. Even upon being introduced to an important political leader, we would likely only say, "Pleased to meet you, Mr. President," and shake hands in the same manner as we would with anybody else.

In contrast, think of the Russian-style ceremonial greeting of a visiting hierarch: The faithful approach him much as they would an icon, touching the floor (a "little reverence" or *metania*) and then holding out cupped hands for a blessing. The bishop then makes the sign of the cross and drops his hand into those of the layperson, who kisses it. (In some traditions both priests and bishops are greeted in this manner, even outside a liturgical context. In Europe, a pious greeting to any cleric, even by another cleric, is "Bless, Master/ Father," or the Greek "*Evlogite.*")

While some Orthodox traditions abbreviate this request for a blessing to a simple bow and reaching for the bishop's hand to kiss it, they nevertheless maintain a certain dignity by the special form of the greeting. This is in contrast to some Western traditions where the clergy are regarded not as the "fathers" of the parish or diocese, but as "friends," "facilitators," or even employees, and are often addressed by their given name and treated much like any other member of the congregation. But our Orthodox regard for our hierarchy is such that we even sing a traditional song of welcome to the bishop, "*Eis Polla Eti Despota,*" or "Many Years to You, O Master."

The Orthodox idea of making greetings appropriate extends to the occasion as well as to particular persons. At church, one may exchange greetings of the day with the parish priest at the veneration of the cross after liturgy. The priest says, "Christ is in our midst!" and the parishioner responds, "He is and ever shall be!" or perhaps "Glory to Jesus Christ!" and "His glory forever!" On a saint's day or other feast, one might say, "*S prazdnikom!*" (Slavonic) or, "The joy of the feast be yours!"

While these greetings mostly take place in a formal liturgical setting, it is good to extend this grace-filled custom beyond the temple doors. During Bright Week in particular, it is easy to carry through the Paschal delight of saying, "Christ is risen!" and replying, "Indeed He is risen!" when we wake our children in the morning, or when we meet our fellow Orthodox for social events.

The simple use of seasonal greetings can help us to transform our everyday lives, even or perhaps especially in this electronic age. When we contact our Orthodox brothers and sisters in Christ by telephone, there is no reason not to say, "Christ is born!" or "Christ is risen!" as appropriate, and get the response from them, just as we would in person, perhaps after first saying, "Hello, Katherine, this is Donna," to identify ourselves. Parish answering machines can hold a seasonal salutation for callers, perhaps with appropriate music in the background. I have even added the usual greetings to the template file for a business letter on my computer—though maybe it would be better for my own habits if I typed out the words individually each time!

I will do so now, for while the world is madly shopping and partying and writing out "Christmas" cards, you are perhaps sitting down with these words in Advent, waiting for the Christmas season when you can say, "Christ is born!" and "Glorify Him!" So until then I say to you, "Christ is in our midst!" and imagine your reply: "He is and ever shall be!"

November 21
Entry of the Theotokos into the Temple

Architecture of the Soul

I HAVE THE MOST WONDERFUL little book, *Then and Now*, by Stefania and Dominic Perring. Its coil binding brings together photographic prints of majestic architectural ruins from around the world ("Now") with transparent overlay pages showing archaeological reconstructions of the buildings as they used to be in their heyday ("Then"). Perhaps not surprisingly, many of these ancient buildings were religious structures—the Temple of Amun-Re at Karnak in Egypt, Cambodia's Bayon temple of Angkor Thom, the sacred Pyramid of the Moon at Teotihuacan in Mexico. It is fascinating to gaze at the reconstructed magnificence of these monuments on the transparent overlays, then to flip the page and see the ravaged remains that are still left standing today.

Perhaps the most striking contrast in the entire book is the entry for the Second Temple, the Temple Herod the Great built in Jerusalem in 20 B.C. The Babylonians looted and destroyed the first temple, Solomon's, in 586 B.C., but it was rebuilt and rededicated some fifty years later when the Jews returned from their captivity. It does seem that the Ark of the Covenant, which contained the tablets of the law, was no longer there—destroyed, according to some, or, according to Ethiopian tradition, borne secretly to safety.

In 20 B.C. Herod the Great, unpopular with his people because of his links with the Romans, tried to boost his reputation with a massive rebuilding scheme, refashioning the Temple in a Hellenistic style—going so far as to place the Greco-Roman symbol of a golden eagle above its door, which was soon (predictably) torn down by an angry mob. Only a few decades of unrest followed before ending in A.D. 70 with the Romans breaking the siege of Jerusalem and razing Herod's splendid gold-and-marble pile to the ground. Since the seventh century the famous mosque, the Dome of the Rock, has crowned the former temple site, and all that remains from Herod's day is the outer precinct wall, now the famous Wailing Wall that is the focus of Jewish pilgrimage.

Architecture is one of the enduring arts/sciences that marks an advanced civilization. We take architecture for granted, living in our twenty-first-century skyscraping cities, but how well the ancients knew its significance, in the days when few structures stood more than a single story high. No wonder the builders of the Tower of Babel were so excited about their project that they fell into the hubris that declared, "Let us build ourselves a city, and a tower whose top *is* in the heavens; let us make a name for ourselves, lest we be scattered abroad over the face of the whole earth" (Genesis 11:4).

A piece of massive architecture, especially a religious one, is a declaration of national wealth and power, a symbol of a way of life, and a focus of popular unity. Living in the Western world in nations without a state religion, it is hard for us to understand just how large a temple loomed in the daily lives of the ancients. Yet any little parish can get a hint of it when it comes to building their own local "temple." The sacrifices and teamwork required to build and maintain a building naturally bind folks together.

Ironically, the Twin Towers of the World Trade Center, many times taller than the Tower of Babel could ever have been, have created more national unity among Americans in their destruction than when they stood tall. But the Temple of God's people, unlike the symbolic architecture of any earthly nation, is an immaterial and eternal Temple, only faintly reflected in the largest and most splendid of church buildings.

Herod's Temple was the one familiar to Joachim and Anna, the parents of Mary, Our Lord's Mother. His building program must have been in progress just about the time this devout couple knew their prayers for a child had been answered. The *Protoevangelion of James*, a second-century A.D. document, brings us a symbolic narrative of the life of the Theotokos, who was destined to give birth to God in the flesh. The author of this book, who wrote well after Herod's Temple had been destroyed, uses the language of poetry to paint a picture of the new spiritual reality anticipated by celebrating the Feast of the Entry of the Theotokos into the Temple on November 21.

The themes of the *Protoevangelion* are taken up by the liturgical texts for the Feast. It may look at first glance as if the Feast is meant to parallel the Feast of the Meeting of Our Lord (February 2), but there is a very important distinction in emphasis. Where Our Lord's entrance into the Temple showed Him to be the Anointed and Savior of Israel and the whole world (Luke 2:22–38), the Theotokos is revealed as the pattern of the Church and of the Christian soul. She is "both Temple and Palace . . . to be prepared as a divine dwelling place for His coming" (Matins of the Feast, Canticle One).

The young Mary—according to the narrative, only three years old, an innocent child wise beyond her years—is compared to the temple furnishings described in Exodus 37—the candlesticks, the ark, the table of sacrifice, the golden censer. These things are important not in their own right, but only because they hold something else necessary for the worship of God—the Law of God, the incense representing prayer, the Light of God's Spirit, the sacrifices of the faithful.

The beauty and solidity of a church building can be a wonderful testament to the Orthodox faith. But even the most spectacular of these will one day lie in ruins. More lasting is the architecture of the soul built by God to be His own dwelling place. St. Paul tells us that we too are the temple of the Holy Spirit—both as individual Christians (1 Corinthians 6:19) and collectively as the Body of Christ, His Church (1 Corinthians 3:16).

The hymns of the feast bid us enter the Temple with the Mother of God, singing and dancing like virgin attendants leading the procession of a queen. In this Advent season, we can build our souls into fit receptacles for God Himself, if we will live as the Theotokos, with childlike trust in our Savior. To be constantly where Christ dwells—that is, not just in a physical building, but in the eucharistic fellowship of His people as they meet Sunday by Sunday, in the other services of the Church, and together in Christian service or in social gatherings—to be there is to be like our Lord's Mother, in a holy place, a place where we can be fed spiritual food by God's angels.

December 6
St. Nicholas

Priming the Pump of Generosity

SNOW, BELLS, CAROLS . . . and a certain bearded figure, clad in red and white. You already know what this is all about. Santa Claus, a.k.a. Saint Nicholas, provides something of a conundrum to the Orthodox family. We know who he really is—a bishop of the fourth century, a wonder-working ascetic and generous philanthropist, a heavenly friend to be admired, imitated, and called upon in hour of need. The tradition of Nicholas as a patron of children and secret gift-giver goes back to three bags of gold he is said to have thrown into the window of a poor father, whose daughters were in need of dowries.

But in our materialistic culture, the image of Nicholas has become distorted, like the reflection in a fun-house mirror, morphed into the figure of an encourager of greed and gluttony, a harmless and comic character intended to make consumers feel good about purchasing everything from soft drinks to stereo systems.

When our family were evangelical Protestants, we decided to dispense with the fat man in the red suit entirely. Our children were never fed the story about the reindeer on the roof; the presents under our tree came from Mommy and Daddy, grandparents and godparents, to whom thank-yous could be made at once, and whose love and generosity were not dependent upon some code of "good behavior." We avoided the mall when S. Claus and his elves were there, selling the chance for children to have their picture taken with the celebrity.

Of course, for many, this sort of thing is simply a bit of harmless make-believe, a game they play until the children are old enough to grow out of it. But when we became Orthodox and discovered the real Saint Nicholas, a whole new world of seasonal activities opened up to us.

One of the joys of being an Orthodox convert in the West today is that when celebrating feasts, you are not confined to a single strand of ethnic customs—you can pick, choose, combine, and develop, sharing and learning as you go. For us Saint Nicholas has been like that. His feast day, December 6, comes a couple of weeks into the Advent Fast that prepares us for the Christmas feast. His transformation into the Christmas gift-giver has been a gradual one over the history of Western Christianity; in some European countries today, his feast-day is still the chief gift-giving day.

So it occurred to us to prune down the "present-overload" of Christmas Day in our household a little by making St. Nicholas Day the day we gave our children their main gift, saving stockings and gifts from others for Christmas. This had a practical bent to it, too, as often the big gift was clothing for the season.

The real excitement, though, is in our yearly Christmas cookie bake, which has become a Saint Nicholas Day tradition for us. The baking is done as close to the day as we can manage; then on the day itself we secretly distribute the results in decorated bags, signed "from Saint Nicholas."

We aren't always too successful in keeping our identity secret from the recipients. But I will never forget a mysterious Saint Nicholas gift that came to us when we were first married. It happened that I had lost a twenty-dollar bill in the grocery store—quite a bit of money then. But not long after, an envelope marked "From Saint Nicholas" was slipped under our door. Inside was—yes, twenty dollars. We never found out who St. Nicholas's helper was, or whether they knew about our loss. But that unknown person's generosity forever fixed in our minds the *giving* versus the *getting* of the season.

A few years ago, a Canadian retail chain started broadcasting a series of Christmas shopping ads. They encouraged their customers to "Give like Santa, save like Scrooge!"

You would think Scrooge had never learned anything from his adventure with the Spirits of Christmas. The ads portray him as willing enough to give generous Christmas presents, but oh, he still resents the money he has to spend on them!

How different Dickens' portrayal of the conversion of his famous miser: "He became as good a friend, as good a master, and as good a man, as the good old city knew."

The change of one behavior in Scrooge's life, from miserliness to generosity, transformed not just the finances but the whole person of Scrooge. But the pump of generosity does need priming, for we are all too accustomed to grasping and not giving. We want, like the modernized Scrooge in the ads, to have it both ways—to be admired like Santa for magically lavish gifts, while at the same time feeling no pinch in our wallets. But the real Saint Nicholas was able to give so abundantly because he ascetically denied himself.

Saint Nicholas's Advent feast, and the Christmas season he is now so bound up with, offer us excellent opportunities to begin to learn to give in small ways, as we did with our cookies. Church programs such as Christmas shoeboxes of gifts for children in developing countries; a regular basket for offering food bank donations at the church; or a family trip to the store for a gift to an unknown child through the local Christmas bureau—these are just a few of the ways to celebrate with joy the spirit of giving that flows like a fountain through the real Saint Nicholas.

One more point: I think it no accident that Nicholas is commemorated not only on his own feast day, but also on every Thursday of the year, sharing this high honor with the Apostles as does no other saint of the Church. His troparion can be a weekly reminder to share our goods with others in need when we sing: "Because of your lowliness heaven was opened to you; because of your poverty riches were granted to you."

The Christmas season is a good time to prime the pump. But to be truly saintly, we want the flow of generosity to continue throughout the year. Holy Bishop Nicholas, pray to Christ our God for us!

Sunday of the Forefathers

Stories Within the Story

"THE UNIVERSE IS MADE OF STORIES, not atoms," writes the poet Muriel Rukeyser. I am sure she speaks figuratively, not literally. Nevertheless she speaks the truth: the outer reality of the material universe, amazing as it is, pales before the richness and complexity of the spiritual undergirdings of God's creation. God is the Author of the most tremendous Story ever told; and within that Story are many smaller stories, each reflecting some facet of the whole.

God is not finished telling this Story yet, and we ourselves are living inside it. But we can read some of the little stories within the Great Story, and from them draw encouragement and enrichment for our own personal stories. On this Sunday two weeks before Nativity, we celebrate the many outstanding characters in the opening chapters of the Great Story, our Forefathers and Foremothers in Christ who served God in the Old Testament dispensation, taking part in the preparation of the world to receive its own Creator into itself as a little Child.

From Adam to John the Baptist, the hymns of the day praise the numerous individuals who, throughout the history of God's dealings with His people, performed heroic feats in His service. But we read these stories backward, in a sense, for the light of the Incarnation stretches back to illuminate the world even at its murky beginnings.

The Monk of the Eastern Church in *The Year of Grace of the*

Lord points out the foreshadowing of new things in the old stories: "In Abel the first martyr, and the prototype of the Good Shepherd as well as the Sacrificer; in Melchisedek the type of the eternal priest; in Abraham the spirit of faith and the type of the Father; in Isaac the spirit of sonship and of sacrifice; in Jacob free election, patient service and conversion; in Joseph the great features of the Passion and of Christ's redemptive work . . . through the reading of the Prophets the voice of Jesus himself speaks to our hearts."

Among the many others, the three young men in the fiery furnace (Daniel 3:8–30) appear frequently in the texts for this celebration—even more than usual, for they turn up regularly in the seventh and eighth odes of Sunday Matins. Why even more for this particular Sunday? The three men are a reminder of the angels who visited Abraham (Genesis 18:1–12), a Trinitarian symbol; and the furnace is reminiscent of the burning bush of Moses (Exodus 3:1–3), in turn a typological foreshadowing of the virgin womb that can hold the living God and yet not be destroyed. "Thy young men, O Christ, when they were in the furnace which was to them like dew, mysteriously figure Thy birth from the Virgin, which has illumined us without burning us." Here we have a hint of the Feast of the Nativity soon to come.

The stories recounted in the Scriptures thus reflect each other, and reflect parts of that larger Story of God's Love that so loved the world as to send His own Son to us.

Dorothy L. Sayers in *The Mind of the Maker* presents an extensive analogy between the writer or artist at work and the creative work of the Holy Trinity. The work of the human artist or writer she calls "an act of love towards the [artist-creator's] own imaginative act and towards his fellow-beings." Storytelling lies at the very heart of human nature, for we are made in the image of the Great Storyteller, who creates because He loves.

Our poor human stories are tainted with our fallen imperfection, and yet they are not always utterly darkened. C. S. Lewis writes in *Mere Christianity* of the dim reflections of Christian theology often to be found in the mythology of the pagans, and calls these "good dreams." Where ancient pre-Christian cultures tell of a god who dies and rises again, the Christian can see past the pagan agricultural worship to the reality of the God who afterward invaded history as a human, died and rose again. Just as St. Paul reasoned with the pagan philosophers of Athens (Acts 17:16–32), finding support for his arguments in their own works, so we too can find echoes of the Gospel calling to the lost sheep of the world in many unexpected places.

Lewis recounts in his autobiography, *Surprised by Joy*, that he himself was first awakened to his longing for God, without recognizing it as such, through Norse mythology. Little did he know where the echoes in these pagan stories would take him! God, he observed later, is very unscrupulous in what He will use to bring His wandering children to Himself.

If one day God's Great Story were to be made into a movie, then you would have to call the heroes and prophets of the Old Testament "stars," as the hymns of Matins for the Sunday of the Forefathers appropriately declare: "You shone as heaven's lights upon the earth, enkindling the light of piety." Since the verse continues, "You called forth the choir of all creation as you sang to the Master," I suppose that, in the best Christmas tradition, the movie would have to be a musical, too!

Like the best contemporary fiction and drama, the Old Testament presents characters with all their "warts," and does not shrink from such human contradictions as a man "after [God's] own heart" like David who could nevertheless slip and fall into lust and betrayal (1 Samuel 13:14). It is because of this biblical honesty that we know there is hope for us too, flawed and sinful though we are.

The wonderful thing about this Great Story is that we are not to be a passive audience. We may not all be artists and writers, producing famous detective novels or children's books like Sayers and Lewis, but we are all writing our own life stories within the Great Story each day. That is why we need to look for help to these heroic Forefathers, who have trod the path before us. We need sometimes to slay giants as did David—not ten-foot warriors, perhaps, but great trials in our life. We need to obey like Noah; endure like Job;

dance like Miriam or fast and pray like Esther. Their aid can be ours for the asking; their stories our illumination whenever we choose to open the Book of Books.

Sunday of the Genealogy

God's Family Values

"WHAT IS A FAMILY?" Certain social forces in the Western world today seem intent on finding new and ever-broadening answers to that question. But there was a time when the question wasn't even really asked.

Think of the scene near the end of *Fiddler on the Roof,* as the refugees prepare to flee the *pogrom* against their beloved little home village in the Ukraine. "I'm going to stay with my brother in Chicago, America," says Lazar Wolff. "I hate him! But," he adds with a shrug, "a relative is a relative!"

Admittedly, the breaking down of family ties is no new phenomenon. But it is only recently that there have been concerted efforts to normalize it. We have come a long way in the last century from Tolstoy's *Anna Karenina,* in which a woman's desertion of her husband and child ends in madness and suicide, to contemporary books for kindergarten children which portray divorce, single-parenting, and even same-sex parenting partners not just as "real" but as normal and positive.

In the midst of our broken and scattered society, an interesting thing has happened with the proliferation of the Internet: the popularity of genealogy and family history research has mushroomed. People hungry for the sense of belonging they have never known are feverishly searching out their roots, finding long-lost cousins, keeping in touch with relatives by e-mail as they never did with paper post.

What is a family? The so-called "family values" movement has been attempting for some years to facilitate a return to an older definition of family, focusing in particular on the basic nuclear family unit—mother, father, children. Regrettably for a great many people, reality, even in Christian households, falls very far short of the ideal.

Perhaps, then, we can take courage from the fact that when people in Jesus' time trumpeted their assumptions about what a family should be, He gave them a surprising and disturbing response. In the Gospel passage that is read at all the Marian feasts of the Church (Luke 11:27, 28), one of our Lord's audience proclaims, "Blessed *is* the womb that bore You, and *the* breasts which nursed You!"

"More than that," He is quick to respond, "blessed *are* those who hear the word of God and keep it!"

On this final Sunday before Christmas in the Church's seasonal cycle, we devote our attention to the genealogy of Jesus, His earthly ancestors. The Gospel reading (Matthew 1:1–17) is the one with all those "begats." They leave no doubt that when God sent His Son to us, it was into the arms of a family, a family with a great deal of history.

Not all of it is pleasant history—beginning with the fall of Adam. Many of the names are famous for their sanctity, but others we remember for their terrible failures. Yet God was pleased to make them all part of His plan.

"Abraham is our father!" boasted the Pharisees (John 8:39). But Jesus was not fooled by the superficial. Those who believe in the Lord are the true children of Abraham.

St. Paul's image of the tree graft (Romans 11:16–24) tells us how we can become part of God's family, regardless of our own ancestry. We may not be able to trace our fleshly family tree back to the Old Testament, but we are welcomed with open arms into the spiritual family of the Church when we are baptized into Christ.

Just because it is a "spiritual" family, though, does not mean this family has no concrete effect on our daily lives; quite the opposite. Of the early Church it was said, "Behold, how these Christians love one another!" The members addressed one another as "brother" and "sister," and St. Paul spoke of himself as a father in the Lord to those he had converted (1 Corinthians 4:15).

The epistles give us very explicit instructions on how we should help and care for each other in this family of faith, especially for orphans and widows without other family support (1 Timothy 5). And we see this happening in healthy parishes today—especially where members of the church community take under their wings those rejected or estranged from their "natural" families.

Christmas can be an especially troublesome time when it comes to family relations. Many earthly expectations are put upon family celebrations at this time of year, and it can be difficult to enter fully into the spiritual meaning of the feast when our biological family does not share our faith. We need to remember, as we approach the Nativity, that the biblical view of family is somewhat ambivalent. God created families for a good purpose, to nurture and help; yet in this fallen world, the good can become the enemy of the best. Our Lord's most troubling statement even seems to repudiate family ties: "If anyone . . . does not hate his father and mother . . . he cannot be My disciple" (Luke 14:26).

Why would He want us to *hate* our family, when in everything else He says to us He teaches us to *love* others?

To hate in this sense does not mean to harbor bad feelings, but to reject, to choose otherwise. We find it difficult to see how we should reject our families when we live in peace and prosperity. The martyrs have known otherwise, however; some were betrayed by their own families to the persecuting authorities, just as Jesus foretold (Mark 13:12).

Some who heard Jesus' invitation to discipleship gave various family obligations as their excuse for not coming; they needed to wait till their father was dead and buried, they were needed on the family farm, or they had just gotten married (Luke 14:20). We face the same choice today: earthly family, or heavenly?

One wonderful blessing in this hard truth of the Faith is that sometimes it does not need to be either/or. Sometimes instead of choosing between the Christmas services and the family dinner, we can invite the family to join us at church. We can be like St. Andrew, who went to his brother, Peter, and brought him to Jesus (John 1:41, 42).

What is a family? It is a gift from God, whether it is in the providence of our personal genealogy, the values and history passed down to us from our ancestors, or in the blessing of present fellowship. God's family values are not those of this world—but when the Church steps in to minister to the orphans, widows, and wounded; when Christians dare to choose His service even in the face of family opposition; then the Light of Christ shines and enlightens all around.

Part III

God Incarnate

December 25
Nativity of Christ

The People That Sat in Darkness

"NOW, I WANT YOU ALL to turn your lights out," said our guide. Each of us obediently reached up to the little switch behind the lamp mounted on top of our helmet, and eased it closed. One by one the lights died, until finally we sat listening self-consciously to our own breathing, and to the drip of water in the 8°C chill of the cave. The dark was almost palpable around us.

After a few moments our guide said, "Now put your hand in front of your face. Can you see anything at all?"

I waggled my fingers in front of my eyes—at least, I think that's where I waggled them. We were many yards below the surface, and around one or two bends; the entrance to the cave itself was sealed by a steel door to control access and prevent vandalism. Not a particle of light could possibly penetrate to our location, yet a few members of the party hesitantly said that they thought that *maybe* they could see *something*.

The guide kindly disabused them of this delusion. Whatever power of suggestion might have worked on their imaginations, it is impossible to see without light.

Thus St. Matthew quotes the prophecy of the coming of the Messiah: "The people who sat in darkness have seen a great light" (Matthew 4:16; Isaiah 9:2). Sitting there amongst the sharp, rough stones of the cave, we barely had time to get a hint of how terrible a real, complete darkness might be. We switched our lights on a moment later and continued our explorations, the beams illuminating the shimmering limestone formations adorning walls and ceiling. Without light, we would have remained blind to the majestic beauty God had created in that hidden place deep underground. And more, without light, a person could not even begin to imagine which way to go in that cave. You wouldn't know, if you could manage to crawl ahead, whether you were headed for the entrance, or whether at any moment you might misstep and slip, helpless and hopeless, downward and deeper into the cave system.

Light and life go hand in hand. Without light, nothing can grow, physically or spiritually. In high northern latitudes, there are dreadful winter days when the sun does not rise at all. In such countries, health care officials have noted an extremely high instance of Seasonal Affective Disorder (SAD), a sometimes severe form of depression that is alleviated chiefly by exposure to sunlight.

Even in the more southerly realm of the Ancient Roman Empire, where the seasonal contrast was not so marked, people felt the dreariness of winter darkness. Astronomy, however, as in other ancient cultures, had determined the turning point of the year, at which the longest night holds the world in its grip, only to be forced once more to relinquish its grasp as the solstice passes and the days begin to lengthen once again. As those dark winter days concluded the old year and hope stood on the horizon of the new, the Romans celebrated the feast of *Sol Invictus*, the Unconquered Sun, with revels and drunkenness, not unlike many modern New Year's celebrations.

Upon this dark pagan world the gospel broke like the dawn in the first century. "In Him was life," St. John says of the Word who became incarnate, "and the life was the light of men" (John 1:4). So it is no surprise that the Church adopted midwinter as the time to celebrate the Nativity of Our Lord and God and Savior Jesus Christ, the Light of the World.

Halfway across the world from the cave I visited on Vancouver Island this summer lies the Grotto of the Nativity. From at least the time of St. Helen's discovery of the site in the fourth century, this hollow in the earth has been venerated as the birthplace of the Light of the World. Icons show us how this natural cave was used as a stable.

Though I have never made the pilgrimage to Bethlehem myself, I can travel there by faith, through the Gospel accounts, through the liturgical poetry of *The Festal Menaion*, through icons. In a cave beneath the earth, a place hidden from the light of day, was born the One who is a light to lighten the Gentiles, as Simeon proclaimed Him (Luke 2:32). In the Grotto today, ancient icons glow in the candlelight, and the great Star of Bethlehem, a gleaming silver star set in the floor, marks the place of the Holy Birth. It is visited by devout pilgrims and secular tourists alike. Truly, as the Presanctified service tells us, "the Light of Christ enlightens all."

I wonder, though, what the visitor without faith might see there.

Some years ago I read an account of her youthful experience with abortion by noted author Ursula LeGuin. A bright young college student from a well-off family, her panic at finding herself pregnant was quickly allayed when her family easily arranged an abortion for her. She writes with heart-rending eloquence of how she almost literally laid her first-conceived child on the altar of her education and career. Most chillingly, she draws the conclusion that not only wealthy girls like herself, but all, should have easy, uncomplicated access to abortion. After reading the moving account of her *angst*, I regarded the final words of her article with horror: addressing her fellow abortion advocates she says, "Shine, girls. We are the light."

I wonder if Herod pretended, that dark night in Bethlehem, that he was the light. That his slaughter of innocents was for some greater good. It seems probable that he did not bother with such self-justification, accustomed as he was to the bloody internecine power politics of his day. Our Lord, however, did encounter in His ministry those who claimed to be light and to see clearly, when they were no such thing. He called the Pharisees "blind leaders of the blind" (Matthew 15:14). Like the people in our spelunking group, they thought they could see something, when in fact they were in total darkness; worse, they were entirely confident that they could not only see, but give light to others.

Those who sit in darkness are sitting because they dare not move. Unlike the Pharisees, they know they can see nothing, and that they are in danger. They must wait for rescue by Someone who will bring them light. Such were the shepherds that first Christmas.

Far from such meager illumination as the oil-lamps of towns could give in those days, they sat in darkness until the angel of the Lord came in shining glory to bring them the good news.

How strange that, to find the Light of the World, they had to make their way from the darkness of the fields into the darkness of a cave in the earth. Once there, it was the light of faith that enabled them to see more than a baby wrapped in swaddling clothes—they saw what the angel had promised, the anointed of the Lord, the Savior. The One who came to those sitting in darkness, bringing them light.

We too sit in darkness, as the lengthening nights of Advent carry us toward the Feast of the Incarnation. But if we at least know that we are in darkness, then like the shepherds we can sit in faith, waiting for the Light-bringer to rescue us, until we hear at last this joyous message from Matins of the Forefeast of Nativity:

"The star from Jacob has risen within the cave . . . let us see God in swaddling clothes. . . . A Light shall spring forth from the root of Jesse, as the prophet full of light foretold. . . . O Bethlehem, receive the Mother of God: for she has come to thee to give birth to the Light that never sets."

January 6
Theophany

Dragons in the Waters

FROM ANCIENT TIMES, we humans have had a love-hate relationship with water. We cannot live without it; in extreme circumstances, many people can go weeks without food, but rarely can anyone survive more than a few days without water. A cleansing bath gives health and comfort; but give us too much water at once and we drown, overwhelmed by a storm at sea. Timely rains cause the earth to bloom, but a flash flood rushing in torrents down a valley after a long drought destroys everything in its path. Perhaps worst of all, we have always known that the sea's mysterious depths are like the darkness of night: capable of concealing monsters.

Maybe it's that uncertainty that troubles us most, the possibility of betrayal by the deceptively calm waters that harbor beasts like Leviathan, Grendel's mother in *Beowulf,* or the great white shark in *Jaws.*

The residents of Walkerton, Ontario, certainly felt betrayed when a deadly outbreak of *E. coli* in their town was traced to the water supply they had thought safe. A subsequent inquiry laid blame on government cutbacks and careless inspectors; but regardless of the human factors, it was bacteria that sickened many of the residents, killing several. If the inspectors had done their job, they would have detected the "dragons" in those waters—tiny monsters, at the opposite end of the scale to the "great fish" that swallowed Jonah, but equally dangerous and terrifying.

The water imagery in the liturgical poetry of Theophany is some of the most powerful in Orthodox literature. The hymns and prayers of the services elaborate on scripture after scripture about water, till the very pages of *The Festal Menaion* seem drenched. The children of Israel crossing the Red Sea, the prophet Isaiah offering cleansing, baptismal teaching in the Epistle to the Romans, psalms urging the waters to join all Creation in praise of God, dew falling on Gideon's fleece, Jonah and the whale, and of course the Gospel accounts of our Lord's baptism proper to the feast.

But first of all these watery motifs, in the opening hymn of Vespers of the Forefeast, comes an allusion to Psalm 73:13 (LXX): "Make ready, O River Jordan: for behold, Christ our God draws near to be baptized by John, that He may crush with His divinity the invisible heads of the dragons in the waters."

When we remember that Theophany was once the chief baptismal feast of the Church, it comes as no surprise to meet with verses like these, from the first canon of Matins: "Let us, the faithful, keep ourselves safe through grace and the seal of baptism . . . this divine washing unto regeneration shall be our Exodus."

The water of baptism changes us. We are so familiar with this concept, we take it for granted. We know it is about washing away our sins. Theologians have long ago pointed out that Christ Himself, sinless and divine, had no need to undergo this cleansing rite that John the Baptist offered prophetically to those who were penitent. Our Lord entered the waters of the Jordan in humility, sharing our human nature but not our fallenness. Yet the icon of the Feast, and the hymns about the "dragons in the waters," establish at once that this Feast is less about Christ's humility than about His divine power. Naturalistic Western art may show the Lord humbly kneeling beneath the outstretched hands of John, the water falling through the Forerunner's fingers onto the Savior's head; but an Orthodox icon of the Theophany offers us instead the strange and powerful image of our Lord standing, apparently on the waters as He did in the Gospel account of His walking on the Sea of Galilee (Mark 6:48).

Different icons of the Theophany may show a number of

allegorical figures which demonstrate Christ's divine power over the waters of the natural world and their spiritual counterparts— sometimes a female one signifying the sea, or a male one representing the Jordan, both referring to God's Old Testament power over the waters, when He caused them to flee before His people (Psalm 114:3–5). From Christ too these iconic figures recoil in dread. A fish sometimes stands for the sea monsters, or, more graphically, the heads of serpents are shown being crushed beneath Jesus' feet.

There it is. The water of baptism changes us—but in *His* baptism, it is *Jesus* who changes the spiritual nature of water itself, forever. "Now the nature of the waters is blessed by Thy baptism in the flesh" (Compline Canon 9, Forefeast of Theophany).

Christ purges the waters of their monstrous infestation. Hear these thrilling words placed in our Lord's mouth in the Sixth Hour of the Eve of Theophany: "I am in haste to slay the enemy hidden in the waters, the prince of darkness, that I may now deliver the world from his snares."

The annual service of the Great Blessing of the Waters at Theophany celebrates this change in the nature of water and triumph over evil worked by the manifestation of Christ's divine power: "He who alone is clean and undefiled was cleansed in the Jordan that we might be made clean, sanctifying us and the waters, and crushing the heads of the dragons in the waters."

Water without Christ remains a symbol of hidden evil. In the film *The Beach*, a group of people form a utopian community on a hidden South Sea island. The settlement beside the dazzling waters of the tranquil lagoon seems to be paradise itself, until one of the men is attacked by a shark. But there is no grace or transformation in this irreligious, self-centered, pleasure-seeking community, and the hidden monsters of the human spirit soon churn their way to the surface.

The members of the group will not take their wounded comrade to a mainland hospital, lest their secret paradise be exposed, and so, lacking the means to heal him, they finally carry him some distance away from their little settlement so that his cries of agony will not disturb their languid days of swimming, sunning, and playing. The long swim that leads the film's main characters to the island is only a pseudo-baptism, an initiation into a life of surface beauty and pleasure whose depths are infested with monsters.

This is why we bless water, and use it to bless other things—our homes, our selves, icons, candles, the harvest, livestock, even cars. It is a powerful proclamation of the sovereignty of Christ over the evil powers that lurk beneath the surface of the world around us.

At this time of year it is customary not only to bring home little bottles of holy water, but also to invite our parish priest to bless our homes with the sprinkling of water and singing of the Theophany troparion. As we face the year ahead in this world of hidden dragons, let us not neglect these healthful and sanctifying customs of blessing our lives with the waters of Theophany.

January 7
Synaxis of John the Baptist

Spiritual Math

I'M ONE OF THOSE PEOPLE with a severe math phobia, seriously top-heavy on the right side of the brain. You don't want to see the shape of my household account books—in fact, neither do I. Household account books have numbers in them, and numbers make my eyes glaze over. Thankfully, I'm not much into spending, so we mostly seem to have some money left over at the end of the month instead of vice versa. (At least, that's what the bank's computer tells me.)

I may get kind of hazy in the second half of the twelve-times table, but at least I do understand the difference between adding and subtracting. Oddly enough, there seem to be a lot of people who can juggle numbers like circus performers juggling balls, and yet their brain somehow shorts out when it comes to applying the principles of adding and subtracting to the things they spend their lives doing.

I guess we can't entirely blame these poor, rat-race–trapped postmoderns; they've grown up in a post-Christian society, and have probably never heard our Lord's parable about the rich man who decided to pull down his grain storehouses so he could build bigger ones (Luke 12:16–21).

This man had done the math, and was quite sure expansion was the way to go. But he didn't understand that spiritual mathematics work on a very different principle. "What will it profit a man if he gains the whole world, and loses his own soul?" (Mark 8:36).

Jesus called this man a fool, because he was not even going to live to see those bigger storehouses built; instead, he was going to be judged on how little he had shared with the needy of the wealth he already had.

We can increase in a lot of ways materially, only to decrease spiritually. Take that other parable about investment, the parable of the talents, remembering that it isn't really about money (Matthew 25:14–30). The unwise servant had buried what his lord had given him to invest. He thought he was gaining something even more important than additional money—security. He was afraid of losing the money on the market. But his lord was not pleased. Instead of security, the man should have valued obedience. If he had at least dared to bank the money, he would have had a small profit to show—and, more importantly, would have gained the approval of his lord.

In his book *Celebration of Discipline*, Quaker author Richard Foster talks about what we can gain when we give something away—freedom. Perhaps even more than the useless storehouses of the rich man, the sheer clutter of things in our (luxurious, by global standards) homes and the constant restless activity of our modern lives ensnare us by adding more than we can handle—and subtracting things we don't even miss because we have never known them.

John the Baptist, whose *synaxis* (attached feast) is celebrated the day after Theophany, knew well the workings of spiritual math. His way of life was such as to subtract nearly everything the world values, allowing the addition of things with eternal value.

The first thing that decreased for St. John, when he went out into the wilderness, was comfort. He dressed in rough animal skins rather than civilized "soft garments" (Matthew 11:8), endured the extremes of temperature in the desert, and lived on a subsistence diet of locust beans and wild honey—which he would have had to raid from the bees!

He also lost societal approval. The same kinsmen who thought Jesus was "out of His mind" (Mark 3:21) were not likely any more impressed with his cousin John's wild-man routine; and when he started offering good Jews baptism—a rite previously reserved for "unclean" Gentiles—he attracted the disapproving attention of the respectable elements of society, the scribes and Pharisees.

And unlike the timid servant who buried his talent, John voluntarily gave up his personal security for what to worldly eyes was a very risky investment indeed. Putting all his faith in the God who had called him to be His prophet, he braved the wrath of Herod to speak the truth. For his trouble he lost first his freedom, and then his head.

To the worldly eye, John's life is one long series of subtractions.

Now let's see what he gained. A man who goes out into the asceticism of life in the wilderness gains first of all some rare treasures: solitude and silence, without which it is hard to hear God's word.

Friends and family might have withdrawn their approval, but John soon gained a band of devoted disciples who listened eagerly to his words about the coming Messiah. Just as Jesus says, those who leave mothers and fathers and brothers and sisters for His sake will receive again mothers and fathers and brothers and sisters a hundredfold (Mark 10:29, 30).

"Whoever loses his life for My sake . . . will save it," our Lord says (Mark 8:35). John is the ultimate exemplar of this saying, last prophet of the Old Covenant and first martyr of the New. At the command of a corrupt ruler, who was egged on by a scheming adulteress, John died violently; his fame lives on in the hearts of Christians around the world, his image enshrined on the main iconostasis of nearly every Orthodox church. In heavenly glory now he joins the angelic praise of God, and hears the prayers of the earthbound faithful.

As St. John the Baptist's ministry was ending and that of his friend and kinsman Jesus beginning, he told his followers, "He must increase, but I *must* decrease" (John 3:30). True as a description of the situation at that one point in time, but true also as a description of the foundational life philosophy of a man who called himself a "voice of one crying in the wilderness, 'Make straight the way of the LORD'" (John 1:23).

Nowadays, the common approach to life is to keep adding

things—bigger homes, more electronic toys—and activities—more advanced education, more professional accomplishments, more thrilling recreation, higher public honors. How wise we would be to start subtracting some of these instead, and seeking the solitude and silence in which there will be room finally for there to be less of us, and more of Him.

February 2
The Meeting of Our Lord in the Temple

Supporting Players

"REMEMBER, CHILDREN—there are no small parts, only small actors," intones the prim and overbearing pageant director in Barbara Johnson's *The Best Christmas Pageant Ever.* Fortunately for the children in the story, she breaks her leg and is replaced. The child actors know better: of *course* there are small parts, and some of the children are perfectly content to have them.

This children's book is a classic because it strikes a chord with most everyone. The world is forever sending us mixed messages, trying to build up our self-esteem and tear it down at the same time. Our schools preach equality, but practice intense competition. Top-achieving sports figures are held up as paragons and role models, some of them only to tumble from their pedestals in the wake of drug scandals. Teen movies typically win sympathy for the underdog, the ordinary character, the geek or outsider, who is persecuted by the popular elite. But the actors in these roles never actually have crooked teeth, zits, or an inch of fat anywhere on their body; and the characters almost never find contentment in simply being themselves—the movie blueprint requires that the "plain" girl become prom queen, the clumsy boy make the winning touchdown.

Everyone, it seems, wants to be the star of the show—at pretty much any cost, as the prevalence of drug use in sports clearly tells us. The trouble is, there can only be one winner, as St. Paul says (1 Corinthians 9:24). He tells us to run in such a way as to win that one prize—to go all out, to give everything we have. Of course, he does not mean his image to be a strict allegory—there *is* in fact a prize, a crown of incorruption, for *every* one who runs in good faith. But his focus here is on the training and discipline of the athlete as an image of the Christian—on the running itself, not on the adulation of the audience, nor on one's competitors.

Unlike the drug-using athletes, Paul is content to play whatever part God gives to him—he does not insist on devoting himself to his fellow Jews, which is Peter's role, but instead accepts wholeheartedly his own mission, which is to the Gentiles. He does not care so much about either the conditions under which he labors, or his results—"I know how to be abased, and I know how to abound" (Philippians 4:12)—he leaves those to God, and merely runs his own race in such a way as to win the crown, with discipline and temperance in all things.

The Feast of the Meeting of Our Lord celebrates a short scene in the drama of the Incarnation, as the Christ Child is brought to the Temple to be made a member of the covenant of Israel. And in this episode we see two new players come briefly on stage, not to steal the scene but, in the same spirit as St. Paul, simply to play their own small parts.

Simeon the God-Bearer puts in only the briefest of appearances, and then makes his exit—"Lord, now You are letting Your servant depart in peace . . . for my eyes have seen Your salvation" (Luke 2:29, 30). His role in the play of salvation was mostly to simply wait, throughout his long life; as the Gospel for the Feast tells us, he was "just and devout, waiting for the Consolation of Israel" (Luke 2:25).

The aged prophetess Anna too has little more than a "walk-on" in God's epic drama. In the services for the Feast she is barely there. In the icons we usually see her looking over Simeon's shoulder at the infant Messiah he holds in his arms. Considerable liturgical poetry is devoted to Simeon, but only a few verses acknowledge this amazing lady—and I rather think that perhaps that actually pleases her better than "equal time" would do. The few verses (in the Slavic use) regarding her are quite telling, however: "O daughter of Phanuel, come and stand with us and give thanks to Christ our Savior, the Son of God. . . . Anna, sober in spirit and venerable in years, with reverence confessed the Master freely in the temple."

Anna does not envy Simeon his role as God-bearer, but is content to stand and wait until his part is done and hers has come. Simeon too is content with the completion of his service, leaving Anna to her continuing work, which, St. Luke tells us, was to speak of the Lord "to all those who looked for redemption in Jerusalem" (Luke 2:38).

Not all of us are called to the high-profile positions in the Church either, as St. Paul tells us in his practical treatise on life in the Body of Christ (1 Corinthians 12). "Are all apostles? Are all prophets? Are all teachers?" Obviously we can't have more chiefs than Indians, as the saying goes, and only a very few are called to the priesthood, fewer still to the episcopate. Not many of us will have the gifts and calling to lead the choir, Sunday school, or parish council. But in this we ought to see God's blessing, for those with such callings will have more to account for than the rest of us.

The ministries of Simeon and Anna are much to be desired by us in these latter days; yet how ill-equipped we are for them, because we are used to instant results, and lots of positive feedback telling us that our modest little part really is the stuff of stardom after all, contrary to our own good sense. But God did not ask Simeon and Anna to be stars—only to be faithful, which they were for many long years. Simeon was "just and devout," and Anna surrendered any hope of children by not remarrying after her husband died, choosing instead decades of widowhood in order to be in the temple of God.

I was delighted at a recent writers' conference when the keynote speaker, Bruce Holland Rogers, spoke about the joy of being a "minor writer." He was addressing an audience of some seven hundred people with writing aspirations. His thorough realism acknowledged that almost none of us would become one of the "greats," like Dickens or Tolstoy. We would almost certainly—every one of us, even the bestsellers—be nothing more than minor writers, when all was said and done. And what's wrong with that?

Most of us won't be called to a ministry as great as those of Peter or Paul. Many, many of us will be like Simeon and Anna, with modest parts to play. But if you have ever been in a school play or community theater production, perhaps you know the satisfaction of a supporting role, a brief walk-on, or maybe even working as crew backstage, merely standing and waiting for a cue to ring down the curtain. Sure, you could do *Romeo and Juliet* without Tybalt, without Friar Laurence or the Nurse—but without those supporting players, it wouldn't be the same play.

As John Milton put it in his famous poem "On His Blindness"— "They also serve who only stand and wait."

Part IV

Open to Me the Gates
of Repentance

Zaccheus Sunday

Little People, Great Heights

FEW THINGS CAN BEAT THE APPEAL of a short hero. From the ancient story of David and Goliath to J. R. R. Tolkien's epic fantasy *The Lord of the Rings* (arguably the most influential book of the twentieth century), the small protagonist, who faces terrible odds and scales great heights, rivets our attention and wins our hearts to cheer him on. At the same time, we often can't seem to resist acting out a bullying impulse we would otherwise be ashamed to indulge, by making fun of little people—witness the seventies satirical song "Short People," or the infamous Mini-Me, tiny clone of the *Austin Powers* super-villain Dr. Evil.

I am a little sad about one particular nuance that was lost in translating *The Lord of the Rings* from the page to the screen, during the Council of Elrond scene. In the book, the old hobbit Bilbo—a Halfling, one of the little people of the world—steps forward amongst the tall folk and offers to take on the burden of bearing the evil Ring on its perilous journey to destruction. Boromir, the tough and skeptical warrior, is about to laugh, but stops himself as he sees that not one of the other exalted persons assembled in the Council thinks it a joke. Little fellow that he is, Bilbo has earned their respect by his past deeds. Bilbo, for his part, does not care for a moment about whether he might appear ridiculous, a little person audaciously setting himself forward in the midst of all these great heroes as if he were their equal.

Perhaps it is this mix of humility and audacity that we find so appealing in the small hero. The short hero perhaps does not so easily fall prey to those delusions the rest of us have about our own importance—and at the same time, he is so used to others being larger than he that, like David facing Goliath, he is perhaps less intimidated than the rest of us when a real giant menaces us.

This is confirmed in the experience of a good friend of mine who was born with spina bifida and needs to use a wheelchair. Except when small children are present, he is always, by nature, the shortest person in any room. When a tall new supervisor at his workplace gave his first staff meeting, most of those present sat cowed about the table while the new boss stood looming large, the center of attention. Afterward one of the others remarked to my friend, "But you weren't bothered by him at all! Why not?"

Because, to my short friend, the tall man was no different from the rest of the world. My friend was already used to holding his own with taller people, every single day.

On the final Sunday before we begin to follow *The Lenten Triodion*, the Church turns our attention to that famous short personage from the Gospel, Zacchaeus (Luke 19:1–10). One of the hated tax collectors who gouged their fellow citizens in aid of the Roman yoke, the vertically-challenged Zacchaeus no doubt made an easy target for "short" jokes. The Scripture does not flinch from giving us this ridiculous picture of a despised little man, who scorns any pretense at dignity to scramble up into a tree in order to see Jesus. (Forgive me for interrupting the flow for a moment here, but I just have to say this—don't you want to see Danny De Vito play the part of Zacchaeus in a movie someday? Not just because De Vito is a short actor, but because he knows how to project that mix of humility and audacity.)

In his book *Great Lent*, Father Alexander Schmemann says this Sunday in the Church's calendar is about desire. "A strong desire overcomes the natural limitations of man; when he passionately desires something, he does things of which 'normally' he is incapable. Being 'short' he overcomes and transcends himself. The only question, therefore, is whether . . . the power of desire in us is aimed at the right goal."

So David the shepherd boy becomes capable of killing Goliath with his sling, and the hobbits overcome and transcend their comfort-loving natures and the limitations of their stature to scale the heights of heroism. But the tall warrior Boromir does not have that power of desire in himself aimed at the right goal. He deludes himself that he wants only to protect his people, but in fact the temptation to use the corrupting power of the Ring has already ensnared his mind.

This desire for the "right thing," says Father Alexander, is what Zacchaeus had, for he wanted to see Christ, and so he becomes a symbol of repentance, heralding for us the approach of the Lenten season: "for repentance begins as the rediscovery of the deep nature of all desire: the desire for God and His righteousness, for the true life. Zacchaeus is 'short'—petty, sinful and limited—yet his desire overcomes all this . . . it brings Christ to his home."

Do we wish to bring Christ to our home? Or do we, perhaps, think too highly of ourselves, as did the religious and political rulers of our Lord's day, so that instead He went to the less important and less respectable people, the little folk like Zacchaeus?

We had better be sure we have our desire focused on the right thing, as this Pre-Lenten Sunday invites us to do. And we had better know that if we invite Christ into our home, there may be some dreadful adventures ahead. Little Bilbo the hobbit was rather nervous about adventures—they make one late for dinner, don't you know? He tried to put off the wandering wizard Gandalf and his offer of adventure, but then invited him to tea. And so Bilbo's story ended with him not still a small and inconsequential person, but the hero of a journey that took him to a dragon's lair. He grew and transcended himself to become a person who was taken seriously by a council of the great.

We hear no more in the New Testament of Zacchaeus after the memorable incident of his climbing the tree to see Christ, having Him to his house, and offering to make fourfold restitution to those he had overcharged. I like to think that is because the rest of our Lord's disciples stopped thinking of him as a "little man" and merely counted him one of their number—just one more of the tax collectors and sinners Jesus loved. Or perhaps they realized, more accurately, that they too were little people, people who could only scale the heights if they had a great enough desire to welcome Jesus into their homes and take the chance of a great adventure.

Sunday of the Publican and Pharisee

The Map Is Not the Terrain

I AM IN LOVE WITH MAPS. I belong to the National Geographic Society; my bedroom is decorated with several years' worth of calendars featuring antique map prints; and I even have a lampshade in a map motif. Cartographic renderings of places from Jamaica to Jerusalem tease my imagination as I gaze on them while riding my stationary exercise bike, going nowhere fast.

I've never been to most of the places delineated on these maps. A childhood in Southern Ontario, a little selective vacationing in Great Britain and down the West Coast of the U.S., a short stay in Pennsylvania, and a bleak few years in the empty spaces of north central Saskatchewan pretty well sum up my expeditions beyond the limits of southern B.C., where I now live. I've traveled more than some, less than many. Just enough, in fact, to whet my appetite for more.

Maybe that's why I eagerly devour books like Tim Severin's *Crusader*, W. Hodding Carter's *A Viking Voyage*, and Nicholas Crane's *Two Degrees West: A Walk Along England's Meridian*. If one were to speak in extreme understatement, one might call these books stories of "adventure travel." They are particularly intriguing because they are journeys not only to other places, but also to other times.

Severin, acknowledged master of this category of literature, first became famous with *The Brendan Voyage*, a modern re-enactment of an ocean crossing by a band of fifth-century Irish monks in a skin boat. It was a wild idea, and more than a little dangerous, but had a historical point to prove: that the tale of Saint Brendan's voyage was not merely fanciful legend, but historically likely.

By contrast, Hodding Carter's *A Viking Voyage* is purely adventure for its own sake. Though he did build—or have built for him—a reproduction Viking *knarr*, the North Atlantic crossing and landing at the World Heritage Site of L'Anse Aux Meadows, Newfoundland, was not at all unprecedented. Carter took his unseasoned crew on a trial-and-error trip that was not merely dangerous but downright reckless, and miraculously lived to tell the tale.

Enter Nicholas Crane with a rather less risky but surpassingly daft idea: to walk from the top end of England to the bottom along the meridian, two degrees west longitude.

As Dickens said about Marley being dead—nothing wonderful can come of what I am about to tell you unless you first understand something. Marley was dead as a doornail; and a meridian is as intangible as a memory. More so, perhaps. A memory is something that used to be; a meridian is something that never was. It is a mere conceit, a thing which does not exist. It is an imaginary line.

You will of course find it on the Ordnance Survey maps Crane used to plot his journey. But as Crane's account of his walk demonstrates, the map is not the terrain.

Crane's devotion to the imaginary line led him places where no trail had been made by God, man, or beast. Frequently he found himself walking places where the maps said one thing and reality hit him over the head with another—usually something uncomfortable, threatening, and occasionally humorous, like the map-mandated public bridleway that should have brought him straightforwardly across a stretch of ground in Northumberland. The little line on the map that proclaimed the path suitable for horse and man had neglected to depict the herd of bullocks Crane found himself fleeing at top speed. After hopping the fence to safety—and landing in a pile of manure—he turned to shout at the unimpressed animals, "It's a public bridleway, you—!"

We humans so easily fixate on minutiae, especially if we have it noted down someplace in ink on paper. That was the situation of the Pharisee who stood praying in the temple in our Lord's parable (Luke 18:9–14), looking down his nose on the penitent publican who lay face down (rather like a man who had fallen into a mountain of manure while trespassing on some farm in pursuit of an imaginary line). You can almost see the Pharisee constricting his nostrils at the scent of spiritual uncleanness: "I thank Thee, Lord, that I am not as other men—or even as this publican!"

In the phrase "even as this publican" we have the Pharisee's grudging admission that the publican was in the right place, doing the right thing: he was in the temple, worshipping God. But according to all the markings on the Pharisee's map, the publican hadn't gotten there the right way. The Pharisee made a point of tithing on the smallest herbs planted in his window box (Matthew 23:23) and of not going more than a specified distance on the sabbath. To him, his rigid adherence to the elaborate rules, evolved over centuries as applications of God's Law, far outweighed the plain and heartfelt repentance of the publican and his cry of "God have mercy on me a sinner!"

The difference between Nicholas Crane's lunatic walk down an imaginary line and the Pharisee's clinging to his written regulations is a significant one: while Crane writes with self-deprecating humor of his encounter with the reality not shown on the map, the Pharisee remains in an ivory tower of self-deception. He thinks the map he has really *is* the terrain, and that he himself is righteous, while the publican is not.

Jesus makes it quite clear how mistaken the Pharisee is: "I tell you, this man [the publican] went down to his house justified *rather* than the other" (Luke 18:14).

It's a sobering thought as we prepare to enter Lent, with its sometimes complex fasting regulations. They are a little like an imaginary line on a map. But even Nicholas Crane allowed himself some leeway in his walk down two degrees west, setting a 1000-meter corridor to either side of the meridian to let him make his way around the occasional utterly impassable obstacle.

As this and the other pre-Lenten Sundays show us, the true penitence, humility, and self-knowledge of the prodigal son,

Zacchaeus, and the publican who cries, "Have mercy on me a sinner!" are the proper response to the reality of our alienation from God. They are really walking the terrain, not mistaking it for the map as did the Pharisee.

Sunday of the Prodigal Son

Journey to Forgiveness

I CAME ACROSS A REFERENCE to our Lord's parable of the prodigal son recently in what might seem an unlikely place: a book on writing popular fiction, *Writing the Breakout Novel* by top NY literary agent Donald Maass.

"It has been told in churches for two thousand years," Maass points out. "How many . . . novels will last that long?"

Long ages before our Lord told this tale of a son's desertion and a father's forgiveness, and in the centuries since, stories throughout the world have taken the form of a journey—many of them, like "The Prodigal Son," journeys that lead "There and Back Again." The concept seems to have a universal appeal—perhaps because so many of us have the experience of going out into the world as adolescents, then discovering, like Dorothy in *The Wizard of Oz*, that "there's no place like home."

The story of the prodigal son begins with the son demanding nothing more than what he feels he's entitled to—and *now*. Why, he thinks, should he have to wait for his inheritance?

Ah, adolescents. So charmingly blind to the benefits of delayed gratification! Funny though, isn't it, how like this young man we are—even those of us old enough to know better. We think we know what's best for ourselves, and yet we almost never do.

You have to wonder why the father in the story doesn't hold the reins tighter on his boy. It would be for his own good, after all. But the little punk seems to have his old man wrapped around his little finger. "I want my share," he says, and daddy gives it to him. And off the kid goes to party his money away.

What kind of father could let this happen? Where did he go wrong?

It can't be that good sense and good morals were never modeled or taught at home—after all, look at the older brother. Strong work ethic, and never a disrespectful word from him.

Still, who knows what might have happened if the younger son had been forced to stay home? What chaos might he have caused in the orderly household? How might he have provoked his long-suffering elder brother? Most importantly, would he ever have learned to appreciate what he had?

The father's apparent indulgence instead turns out to be far-sighted wisdom, for there is no way for this boy to learn but by leaving—and losing everything. Nevertheless, it breaks the father's heart to let him go. Day by day he waits with one eye on the road, and when he finally spies the return of his errant son in the distance, he runs to greet him with open arms.

Pity the poor elder son: he does his duty, never complaining, only to find that his worthless sibling's reward for his wild behavior is to receive a royal welcome home. The elder son hasn't been on the journey, and doesn't know through what suffering and humiliation the other young man has gone to learn his lesson. And so he ends up coming off as the bad guy of the story, sulking when the rest of the household is celebrating.

It is to prevent us taking on the role of this self-righteous elder brother that the Church gives us Lent, and this parable is the lesson (Luke 15:11–32) the Church presents to us three Sundays before Lent proper begins.

Throughout the long weeks of the Great Fast, we will voluntarily forgo rich foods like meat and dairy products, thus experiencing in a small way the deprivation that befell the prodigal as a result of his own careless extravagance. We will offer alms, charitable donations, remembering the poverty he knew when he fell so far as to take the job of feeding unclean animals. And we will pray in self-examination, hopefully to "come to our senses" as the prodigal did, admitting we have wasted our Father's good gifts in careless living; and to come to the resolve that we must return home in humility, no longer demanding our inheritance, but begging only to be treated as a hired servant.

The crux of the parable is in its conclusion. We are not to focus, ultimately, on either the elder son's diligence, or the prodigal's return, but on the Father's forgiveness. We do not earn the fatted-calf feast of Paschal joy by our ascetic Lenten exertions, nor by prim and undeviating "good" behavior. Famished, we are bidden as guests of honor to receive a royal feast; bedraggled, to be clothed in righteousness; powerless, to receive the seal-ring of spiritual authority. It is all the gift of a Father whose whole heart is bent upon our return to Him.

As Donald Maass concludes about this wonderful story of stories, "The reason the story moves us is not that the son has repented but that the father has forgiven."

If Lent is to teach us anything, we must never lose sight of this reality. The Church's Lenten discipline is not merely some sort of self-help course for spiritual improvement. It is a journey, sometimes arduous and humiliating, but ultimately joyful, toward the Father's forgiveness.

Sunday of the Last Judgment

Earthquake Preparedness

LENT STARTED WITH A LITERAL BANG for us in 2001: an earthquake hit the Pacific Northwest.

We in the Lower Mainland of British Columbia didn't fare too badly—it was the streets of downtown Seattle that appeared on the TV news, choked with milling people and crumbled bits of buildings. But we did have some minor damage, a couple of schools and factories temporarily evacuated over fears about structural safety.

I was at my computer, as usual, when suddenly the monitor started shaking and the desk seemed to edge sideways. A heavy thump came from the balcony overhead, like a large person jumping and landing there.

And that was all. For a few days the media buzzed about our inadequate regional disaster plans, people traded "what were you doing when" stories, and kids really paid attention to in-class earthquake drills. We all resolved to replace our supplies of purified water, flashlight batteries, and canned goods. And then never got a round tuit.

You know what a round tuit is—a little paper circle with the word "TUIT" printed in the center. Some good friend gives you one, so you no longer have any excuse to procrastinate about the things you keep meaning to do "when you can get around to it."

You both have a laugh, you affix it to your fridge with a magnet, and promptly go back to procrastinating.

We humans are very good at putting things off, so much so that we seriously resent those few of our number who are different. Ask the student who always gets the assignments in ahead of time.

They say there are several levels of learning, that we take in the least when we are merely told something (a voice on the radio telling us to get our emergency kit together); more if we can also see something (a round tuit posted on the refrigerator); and the most if we can actually do or experience something (feeling the earth move under our feet).

What does it take, if the experience of an actual earthquake isn't enough to make us get our act together? I'm afraid there actually may not be any answer. The Scriptures tell us how in the days preceding the Last Judgment people will continue to marry and be given in marriage (Luke 17:27)—in other words, behaving as if not only will their own lives go on in the same way, but succeeding generations will be the same as well. As if no end will ever come.

Perhaps we cannot live always in such constant awareness of the end of all things, but the Church knows we at least need to be reminded regularly. That is why the second Sunday of Lent focuses on the Last Judgment. The Church has a spiritual "earthquake response plan," and offers her members a spiritual "earthquake preparedness kit."

What is this plan? The Scripture tells us how the faithful will be caught up to heaven to be with Christ, singing and worshiping Him forever (1 Thessalonians 4:13–18). And we prepare for this destiny by gathering as the Church to worship Him in this age. As we are warned in the Epistle to the Hebrews (10:25), we should not forsake "the assembling of ourselves together." To be prepared for the sudden arrival of the Last Judgment, we need our clergy to lead us in serving the full cycle of services, to be constantly in corporate prayer; and we lay members need to attend as many as possible of the services offered at our local parish.

Our "earthquake preparedness kit" consists in a number of things, also provided for us by the Church. There is light for dark times in the Holy Scriptures—"Your word *is* a lamp to my feet," says the Psalmist (Psalm 119:105). There is food that does not perish, the Eucharist (John 6:50, 51), offered on Sundays and feast days, and provided also in reserve for the sick and dying. And God Himself is our shelter against the attacks of enemies and sudden disaster.

A wise community supports a complement of emergency personnel all the time, not waiting for disaster to strike before recruiting them. The Church has the monastics to fill this role, so that constant prayer may be made for the rest of the Body.

On this Pre-Lenten Sunday, we have the opportunity to pause and consider these things. But will we pay no more attention to them than we do to a round paper tuit? It is interesting that in Lent the Church allows no "marrying and giving in marriage." The season is designed precisely *not* to be just like our ordinary lives. It would be best if we came out the other end of Lent, not just a few pounds lighter from fasting, but with some permanent change in our attitude.

The resident of an earthquake zone who at least sets himself a date to renew those water supplies has taken one step in the right direction. Human nature being what it is, we know many of us will not take all the steps we should. But Lent comes yearly to give us a reminder—and more than a reminder, it also offers assistance in carrying out our procedures. When we do our preparation as a community, encouraging one another, we have a much better chance of success than we do at home, listening to the voice of some media spokesperson telling us we "should" do this list of things.

The Church's threefold preparedness program of prayer, alms, and fasting is meant to be enacted in community, not in isolation. Parishioners can assist each other by praying together, and praying for each other; sharing the duties of Lenten meals after Presanctified Liturgies; going as families to a preplanned, unhurried time of confession; organizing charitable ministries or funds so that individuals may give their alms through the local parish.

I admit it—my chlorine-disinfected emergency water supply is still sitting in the garage, overdue for replacement. But I rarely miss a church service, especially in Lent.

Forgiveness Sunday

Exercising Forgiveness

I HATE EXERCISE. IN THE EIGHTIES, I lived in a location where the temperature dipped to 30° below in winter, so instead of the walks I preferred for keeping in shape, I had to jump on the then-new aerobics bandwagon. To me, jouncing around a gym to the twang and thump of country rock with a bunch of other post-partum women, all of us wearing leg warmers and body suits in shades like lime green and neon orange, was a little like being in a *Far Side* cartoon with the caption, "Hell on April Fool's Day."

Scratch the eighties accoutrements, and exercise still seems a shade too close to eternal torment to me. It isn't just the huffing and puffing and sweating and aching—it's the meaningless repetition, like the mythical Sisyphus rolling his boulder up the hill, only to have to start over for the millionth time when it slips down to the bottom.

What a relief to move to a larger center in a civilized climate, where I could walk in the park and study martial arts.

Last year, though, I had a persistent ankle injury. When rest didn't do the trick, x-rays finally revealed an old break I never knew I had, and I was sent for physiotherapy to strengthen my ankle and help it recover.

The clinic assigned me my own personal slave driver—er, exercise therapist—who helped me set up a program. Stretching, strength, endurance exercises with big blue rubber bands. "Twenty repetitions, both feet," this Teutonic lady commanded. "Ten repetitions, ze bad foot. Increase to fifteen!"

Riding a stationary bike, working a stair-stepper, balancing on a trampoline. *Increase!* The home version I was assigned employed less sophisticated equipment, but still added up—to fifty minutes of grueling, wearying, repetitive, stultifyingly boring *exercise*. Twice a day.

"It vill hurt," my angel of the gym informed me. "As long as it is not ze bone, just ze muscle, I dunt *care* how much it hurts."

Well, *that* was starting to sound familiar. Anybody remember their first time at Forgiveness Sunday Vespers?

The Rite of Mutual Forgiveness with which we begin our Lenten discipline is perhaps the most dramatic of all Orthodox ceremonies. This deceptively simple rubrical description appears in *The Lenten Triodion*:

> The priest stands beside the *analogion*, and the faithful come up one by one to venerate the ikon, after which each makes a prostration before the priest, saying: Forgive me a sinner. The priest also makes a prostration before each, saying the same words; and then the other receives his blessing and kisses his hand . . . the faithful may also ask forgiveness of one another.

A more intimate view of a particular Forgiveness Sunday in a particular community comes from Frederica Mathewes-Green's *Facing East*:

> One at a time I bow to people I worship with every week, looking each one in the eye, men and women, children and aged. Each interchange is an intimate moment, and I feel on the wobbly border between embarrassment, laughter, and tears. Just to pause and look at each fellow worshiper for a moment, to see the individual there, is itself a startling exercise. . . . Down the line, as worshipers dip and bend, embrace and move aside, it looks like a dance, a dream-paced country dance laced with dreamy smiles.

But neither source mentions a certain unavoidable fact about the Rite of Mutual Forgiveness: *it vill hurt* . . .

I'm not just talking about those previously unused thigh muscles that are going to stiffen up next day like the Tin Woodsman's when his oil can runs out. Forgiveness hurts, both giving and receiving, because it is therapeutic. No pain, no gain.

Still, it would hurt less if we were more accustomed to practicing it diligently all the time, wouldn't it? Perhaps, like me, you've gone to confession feeling rather silly to say with a sigh, "Father, I've done it again. I've committed the same old sins as last time. And the time before that . . ."

But we know we need the healing power of forgiveness that we receive in the absolution. Coming to confession at preset intervals sometimes seems like a meaningless exercise, but in reality, like a regular routine in the gym, it strengthens us.

I can't say for sure that my ankle is 100 percent healed yet, even though I'm finished going to the gym. (I did, however, discover how to counteract the mind-boggling boredom of doing ten-of-these-for-that-many-seconds-each in my home program: I started doing the counting on my fingers instead of in my head, while saying the Jesus prayer. I sometimes lost count this way, but I came through the exercise session with a more contented spirit.)

In the same way as an injury is not always healed at once by therapy, forgiveness is a process that extends well beyond the ceremony at Vespers. But that does not make the ceremony itself a meaningless exercise. The pain of our spiritual injuries may continue for some time even after we embrace those who caused them. We may leave the church this Sunday still bearing some of the same character flaws that caused us to offend others, so that we needed to make those prostrations towards them.

The orthopedic surgeon who sent me to the exercise therapist told me that if all other measures failed, my ankle might need surgery. Call me a coward, but I preferred the exercise program. . . . In the same way, the church graciously provides us such exercises as Forgiveness Sunday and regular confession, to spare us a more painful eventuality.

So let us sing with the choir the hymn that foreshadows Pascha at this service that ushers us into Lent:

"Let us call brothers even those that hate us, and forgive all by the Resurrection!"

Part V

Lent, the Great Fast

First Week of Lent
Canon of St. Andrew

Only the Penitent

"ONLY THE PENITENT MAN shall pass," Indiana Jones mutters to himself. He is standing at the entrance to the cave containing the Holy Grail and puzzling over this clue gleaned from an ancient manuscript. Suddenly he drops to his belly and begins crawling along the forbidding passage. His advance triggers a booby trap, but the deadly scythe-like blade whizzes harmlessly over his head as he passes by the macabre remains of the proud and unsuccessful pilgrims who have preceded him. The penitent man goes humbly, on his knees . . .

A popular, worldly Hollywood adventure, you say. Real penitence is "spiritual." Ah, but we Orthodox should know better than to think "spiritual" encompasses only the mental or emotional. That is why one of our first and continual Lenten duties is to perform the prayer of St. Ephraim, beginning with several places in the penitential Canon of St. Andrew on the evenings of the first week.

And we do perform, not just recite. Harrison Ford might have recited Indiana's lines for the scene above while he was learning the script, but the performance in front of the camera involved more than the words.

"O Lord and Master of my life, take from me the spirit of sloth, despair, lust of power and idle talk . . ." With these words we perform our first prostration, making the sign of the cross as we name each of the four sinful spirits, then falling to our knees and bowing our faces to the ground.

Sloth. A more archaic and funnier-sounding word than simple "laziness," but long use has given it theological and moral connotations lacking in the alternative. There is no doubt that in sloth we speak of a sinful passion, not some slight personality flaw. Its remedy is in action, in work, and thus we do not stand idle before its onslaught, but perform the work of a prostration.

Despair is sloth's corollary. To weasel out of the need to do work, instead we say, "What's the use? I can't get control of my temper; the fast is too hard for me; I can't help giving in to sexual sin because of how I feel." Despair is dishonest, and does not acknowledge God's sovereign power. Again the medicine for such a spiritual illness is in the prostration, for it is both an active work and a bowing before God's omnipotence.

But in our shrinking from penitence, we may turn in a different direction altogether from that of sloth and despair. If it is the lust of power that most tempts us, we go about like the Pharisee whose tale is told in the pre-Lenten lectionary. Far from despairing in the fight against sin, we stand proudly and look down on the publicans around us, deluding ourselves that our own righteousness is keeping us in control of our lives. What is more, we begin to expect God to share our view. The prostration cuts the Pharisee down to size by bringing him to the same level as the publican.

If we vanquish all these heinous passions, still there remains another possibility, that of idle talk. But how terrible could this be? Wouldn't one have to indulge in a great deal of idle talk before it would be really sinful? But we are taught, "Be still, and know that I *am* God" (Psalm 46:10). In our world of machinery and constant electronic noise, church is one of the few places we can come to be silent. Yet people will often chat sociably together before, after, and even during the service, to the detriment of their fellow members and their own souls. But when we are making prostrations, the whole congregation senses more strongly the solemnity that demands our silence; and bowing our faces to the floor removes the likelihood of our distracting our neighbors, or being distracted by them.

Of course a prostration in itself will accomplish nothing. One can look around at a Lenten service and see some awkward and half-hearted in their performance, others perfunctory and apparently thoughtless. Still others may bow ostentatiously, for the approval of man and not of God.

We should keep in mind the story of the little girl who kept standing up in her chair at the dinner table, finally to be forced to her seat by her father. "Well," she said, folding her arms defiantly, "I may be sitting down on the outside, but I'm standing up on the inside!" Our prostrations must be both on the outside and the inside.

This first verse of St. Ephraim's prayer leads us into the beginning of penitence by attacking four cornerstones of sin in our lives. The second verse carries us further, bringing penitence to fruition by replacing vice with virtue: we pray for the spirit of chastity, humility, patience, and love. And here again we can take a cue from Indiana Jones. Having escaped the terrible traps in the passage of humility, he stands up to see a chasm gaping at his feet, and remembers that the next clue instructs him to take a step of faith.

That too is how we receive these virtues and fulfill our penitent pilgrimage, and the next prostration in the prayer of St. Ephraim is our act of faith. To prostrate oneself before a king in biblical times not only showed humility; it was also an act of faith and trust, putting oneself completely at the mercy of the monarch, who had the power to have the supplicant's head struck off then and there. If we bow humbly, will we be ground into the dust? If we keep silent, will we find God's words too dreadful to bear?

So Indiana Jones steps out into what looks like a fall to certain death, and only then feels and sees the previously invisible bridge bearing him up safely.

Humility begets faith. This is the process of penitence. Indiana's final test in his quest for the Grail is to be confronted with a thousand cups from which to choose; to drink from the true Grail will give life, all others, death. Already having learned humility and faith, he chooses correctly the simplest cup, and drinks. Humility and faith lead to clear vision—of self, others, and God. And so it is that St. Ephraim concludes his Lenten prayer, "Grant me to see my own sins and not to judge my brother, for Thou art holy always."

And why must we make a prostration again at this point, when we have learned all this already? Because the process is cyclic, even as the appointed days and weeks and seasons of the Church repeat endlessly. We learn, but do not learn, and must end as we began, with humility. Only the penitent will pass safely through all the traps that lie ahead this Lent, and in this life.

Wednesdays and Fridays of Lent
Presanctified Liturgies

Is It Soup Yet?

THERE IS NOTHING MORE LIKE LENT than soup. I am reminded of it most strongly on the evenings when we have a
Presanctified Liturgy. Our parish custom is to have a sign-up sheet,
so we can take turns bringing soup to break our fast afterwards. It's
always very ascetic, of course—these are not soups with a cream
base, or a meat broth, but something made of some kind of beans
or lentils, served up with nourishing bread. So simple, and yet nothing could taste better, or be more satisfying and revivifying, after a
full day's fast and a long solemn service of standing, singing, and
prostrations.

Each soupmaker has her own specialty, prepared in her own
unique way—yellow pea with carrots and celery, curried seafood,
the old standby lentil with onion and tomato. But whatever else
goes into the pot, you can't get away from the fact that soup, like
people, is mostly water. And if you make a bean-based soup, you'll
notice that the first thing you do with your legumes is baptize them.

Lent seems to me to be a spiritual soup—something that nour-
ishes us and revives us, by a combination of various ingredients
blended over heat.

There are certain basic ingredients the Church prescribes in her
recipe for the spiritual soup of Lent: the most important, like water
in material soup, is prayer.

We ought to be in prayer like fish in water, all the time; but life and our human nature being what they are, we tend to stay in the shallows. Lent gives us the opportunity to dive deeper—to develop a prayer rule if we have not had one, to solidify and expand upon it if we have one already.

Then we have alms and fasting—rather like the legumes and other vegetables that give soup its substance. It is one thing to pray for spiritual progress for ourselves, or help for those in need; it is something more to take the actions of fasting and almsgiving that become the vehicle for God to answer those prayers. Some families like to tie alms and fasting together by depositing the money they save through eating more simply into a fund for the relief of those who may not always have enough to eat.

We have our liquid and solid ingredients in the pot—now it's time to apply heat. This comes in the form of attendance at the Lenten services, beginning with Forgiveness Sunday. Believe me, if you have not yet experienced it, there is plenty of heat to be had when you approach each of your fellow parish members in turn with a prostration and embrace of mutual forgiveness. This is good, but you want to keep a constant temperature going, and habitual attendance at the extra services of Lent—the Canon of St. Andrew, the Presanctified Liturgies—can help us keep on track throughout the fast.

They say a watched pot never boils. So we have to be judicious when we stir things up by the self-examination we do before confession. Then again, if you leave it sit too long, soup will get burnt on the bottom . . . I don't think we want that to happen to our souls!

These basic ingredients of Lent will provide all we need to feed our souls during the Fast. But like the spices added by creative cooks, there are additional things you may find appropriate to your own or your family's unique practice of Lent. These could include doing special readings; giving up entertainments and treats; or working on our own particular weaknesses. When in doubt, consult your local expert cook—that would generally be your priest, but it would do no harm also to swap tips and "recipes" with your friends, especially the more experienced Orthodox Christians.

I have a confession to make: I am not a soup lover. After

Presanctified Liturgy, I line up to fill my bowl like everybody else, and swallow the warming liquid with gratitude. But I rarely go back for seconds.

Thank goodness no-one expects me to go back for seconds of Lent! Certainly, we have other fasts throughout the year, but none is so strenuous, spiritually and physically, as the Great Fast. But like a lovingly tended homemade soup, it provides for us many good and nourishing things in a single pot.

First Sunday of Lent
Triumph of Orthodoxy

Icons Not Made with Hands

LENT: THE TIME OF REPENTANCE. Each Sunday of the Great Fast has some sober dedication to remind us of this constant theme of our pilgrimage. The mid-Lent meditation on our Lord's Cross; the spectacular asceticism of Mary of Egypt; the theology of Gregory Palamas, champion of the Jesus Prayer *(. . . have mercy on me a sinner)*; the wise Elder John's guide to spiritual discipline, *The Ladder of Divine Ascent*—all of these openly preach contrition for sin and humility before God and man.

Yet the first Sunday of the season appears, at first glance, to defy this pattern of penitence. The Sunday of the Triumph of Orthodoxy celebrates unabashedly the eighth-century victory of the Orthodox theology of Christ's Incarnation over the iconoclasts who denigrated His humanity and wished to destroy the icons. God, who was once invisible, indescribable, undepictable, consented by His Incarnation as a man to become depictable. On this Sunday in Lent, therefore, the images of Our Lord and God and Savior Jesus Christ, and His saints with Him, glitter in vesperal light, held aloft in splendid procession, while troparia in many languages soar joyously to the domes of churches throughout the world.

It is, of course, for historical and not thematic reasons that the celebration of this decisive victory over heresy finds itself placed on the First Sunday in Lent. Yet we need not dismiss this as a mere accident and insignificant, for there is something very appropriate about meditating on the Image of God at the beginning of a penitential season.

Much has been said and written in recent years about icons—their beauty, their heavenly qualities, the prayer and meditation that must go into their writing to make them more than mere pictures. They turn up in the media far more often than was the case ten years ago, almost having become trendy among Christians of widely diverging backgrounds.

Yet in this same period we have seen a previously unparalleled increase in focus upon the self. "*My* hurts, *my* self-esteem, what works for *me*," is the cry of a world that no longer honors others before self. The film *Blast from the Past* had a fascinating comment to make on this phenomenon. Brendan Fraser plays a young man born in the early 1960s and raised in a sealed fallout shelter by somewhat eccentric parents, who imbue him with values that predate the sexual revolution and the "Me" generation. Not surprisingly, when Fraser emerges into the surface world thirty-five years later, his behavior astonishes the inhabitants of the 1990s.

Interestingly in a modern film, Fraser's babe-in-the-woods character is not depicted in a way that condescends to his innocence. Instead, another character reveals his reaction to Fraser with all the awe of a man who has had an epiphany: "He explained to me that being polite isn't acting snobby—it just shows respect and consideration for other people!"

The Psalmist cries, "Against You, You only, have I sinned" (Psalm 51:4). But in what did his sin against God consist? Precisely in sin against his neighbor, who is made in the image of God—an icon not made with hands, we might say. If we really believed that our fellow human beings were made in the image of God, wouldn't we be polite to them, at the least? Wouldn't we be horrified at ourselves to be caught snapping in impatience at the walking, talking icons God Himself has written—sometimes, indeed, under the very eyes of those icons we do honor, on the walls and iconostasis of the sanctuary?

But it goes farther than this, much farther. We humans, even those of us who call ourselves Orthodox Christians, dishonor, deface, and even destroy God's image every day—ignoring, abusing, betraying, and even killing our fellows.

The holy icons, the ones made by devout and yet merely human hands, have been restored for more than a thousand years now. Though we do hear of the destruction of Orthodox churches in the troubled Balkans, for instance, in Western countries at least we can be grateful that there are laws against such desecration. A vandal who walks into a church and starts swinging away at the images of God and His saints will be sought by police and punished by the courts.

Down the street from the church, however, there is in most cities a place where it is perfectly legal to rend the image of God into an irreparable mass of broken pieces. This place is called a hospital, or perhaps a clinic. The icons so destroyed are not ones made with human hands, but by God Himself. They are infants in the womb, just as our Lord Jesus Christ once was.

The Orthodox who lived in the troubled years of the Iconoclast controversy did not rest until they saw the Image of God restored to honor. We their successors in this new millennium can do no less. Here we can see that the theme of celebrating God's image is inextricably wound up with repentance after all. If we would not reverence the icons in our churches in hypocrisy, we cannot be silent about the destruction of God's image by abortion.

Not all of us feel that to be arrested for blocking access to a clinic will ultimately help this cause. But all of us, unless prevented by laziness or fear, can celebrate God's image this Lent by taking some other kinds of action. Most of us can attend perfectly legal public demonstrations or pickets. Some can give financial support to pro-life causes. All but the illiterate can write to their elected representatives. All of us should support the dignity of motherhood, both in our attitudes and by providing concrete help to mothers, especially single mothers.

One last action can be taken by all, even small children. Each time you pause before an icon made of paint and gold leaf and wood, remember to pray for the icons not made with hands.

Second Sunday of Lent
Gregory Palamas

Mirror, Mirror

Mirror, Mirror, on the wall,
Who's the fairest of them all?
 —The Brothers Grimm, *Snow White and the Seven Dwarfs*

I DON'T THINK OF MYSELF as particularly vain, yet there must be nearly a dozen mirrors in my house, if you count the ones in the jewelry box lids. I would venture to guess that, apart from the homeless or bedridden, there's hardly anyone in the civilized world who couldn't go this very instant and look at him- or herself in a mirror, mere steps away. In our world of the instant broadcast, music videos, and omnipresent cameras, concern with personal appearance has reached a fever pitch, and mirror-gazing has become second nature to us. As Paul Simon puts it in his sardonic "The Boy in the Bubble," we are obsessed with "the way the camera follows us in slow-mo / The way we look to us all."

The vanity of mirror-gazing is often thought of as a particularly feminine preoccupation, but the seminal mirror tale, the cautionary ancient myth of Narcissus, involves a young man. Narcissus wandered by a glassy pond and there caught sight of his own fatally beautiful reflection. Dizzy with infatuation, he tried to embrace himself, and so fell in and drowned. The flower bearing his name grew ever after at water's edge, a reminder of the perils of "narcissistic" mirror-gazing.

Our preoccupation with self, and especially with our own image, appears at its most poisonous in the classic fairy tale of *Snow White and the Seven Dwarfs*. Vanity leads to envy, and envy to murder, as the evil queen fixes her attention on the innocent young Snow White's blossoming beauty. Mirror-gazing excludes others from our lives, regarding them as rivals and enemies to be destroyed at any cost.

In the television fairy-tale mini-series, *The Tenth Kingdom*, the theme of the satanically deadly deception inherent in mirror-gazing is shown from yet another angle. Virginia, the heroine of the story, is forced by the evil queen to gaze into a magic mirror. While the queen looks on in serene beauty, Virginia sees herself becoming ugly, and regards herself with loathing and despair. What she does not realize is that the mirror lies. What is really happening, while she stares horrified and enthralled at her own reflection, is that the queen is choking her to death.

We may think ourselves beautiful like Narcissus, or despicably ugly like Virginia's false reflection; but either way, if we focus too much on our own image, we fall prey to the evil designs of our spiritual enemy.

Gregory Palamas, a fourteenth-century bishop and theologian whom we celebrate on this second Sunday in Lent, has a fascinatingly different approach to the mirror. He says in *The Triads*, regarding a mirror or sheet of water, "Receiving the sun's ray, they produce another ray from themselves. And we too will become luminous if we lift ourselves up, abandoning earthly shadows, by drawing near to the true light of Christ. And if the true light which 'shines in the darkness' comes down to us, we will also be light, as the Lord told His disciples."

Gregory's adversaries made heavy weather of the doctrine of Uncreated Light, and he was obliged to meet them on their own rhetorical ground. *The Triads* are a bit daunting to the uninitiated, complex philosophical arguments in an exchange that went on for years, but surely there is something profoundly simple in Gregory's analogy of the mirror reflecting the Sun. We do not need to be intimately acquainted with all the doctrinal ins and outs of "theosis" and "hesychasm" to realize the importance of the "Jesus prayer" Gregory Palamas championed.

"Lord Jesus Christ, Son of God, have mercy on me a sinner." To repeat this prayer is to become a mirror, standing blank and still and silent so that Christ may look into us. We need to stop turning round and round, looking for our own reflection, and let Him shine upon us.

When I was in karate class, I learned a simple little Zen concept that is quite compatible with the teaching of St. Gregory: moon on water. The idea is that a mind and spirit that are still and quiet will reflect reality clearly and accurately. The shining image of the moon on tranquil water has the same light and clarity as the moon itself; but if the water is churned up by wind, the reflection breaks up and becomes meaningless.

"Be still, and know that I *am* God" (Psalm 46:10).

That is what the Jesus prayer helps us to do. If we continue frantically pursuing our own reflection, the inevitable result is death. But if we bow humbly in the stillness of the Jesus prayer, the light of Christ will be reflected in us without distortion. As we sing of Gregory in the second canon of Matins for this day, "You have become a mirror of God, O Gregory . . . you have attained that which is according to God's likeness . . . you have become the glorious dwelling-place of the Holy Trinity . . . you have shone as a light in the world."

The Son of God, He is the True Light, the Sun of Righteousness. He is truly the fairest of them all.

Mid-Lent
Sunday of the Cross

Muddling Through the Middle

I HATE MIDDLES. Most every fiction writer does.

Story has a structure, and it's usually quite easy to know where and how to start a story: with action, with the setting up of a conflict. The hero finds himself in a dilemma—writers call this the "story problem"—and the story is going to be about how he gets himself out of it. There may be a little background information given beforehand, but once you spot the story problem, you know things have really begun to roll.

Readers often keep reading a gripping book far into the night "to find out how it comes out." But writers, when they begin to write a story, most often know already, in a general way at least, where the story will end: around the point where the hero either solves the problem definitively, or perhaps, in a tragic story, fails to solve it.

But the middle—ah, the middle. This is the place where writers frequently find themselves stuck in their own personal literary Slough of Despond. They are weary, frustrated, and don't know which way to go. And perhaps even if you're not a writer, you have experienced a similar feeling in the middle of the Great Fast. Whether it is fairly new to you, or whether you have many Lents behind you, there still comes every year a sticking place, a time when your wheels won't seem to turn, a place that seems so low, you wonder if you're going to be able to climb out of it.

You run out of ideas for meatless meals that your family will eat. The kids are cranky at the evening Presanctified Liturgies and you wonder whether it was such a good idea to bring them. You wake up worn out and can't seem to drag yourself through your prayer rule. You look at the calendar and say to yourself, "How am I ever going to get through that many weeks until Pascha?"

And yet, the middle is the place where things really happen. You can't just jump from beginning to end. The process of Lent—and indeed of life itself—is the instrument by which we get where we are going, the thing God uses to transform us into His divine likeness.

I am often very aware of this when non-Orthodox visitors come to see the Paschal services. They are of course welcome, and we are thrilled to share the joy of the Resurrection with them. We hope that maybe they will react to the glorious Paschal Liturgy as the envoys of Prince Vladimir did when they visited the Great Church of Constantinople: "We knew not whether we were on earth or in heaven!"

But sometimes, even Christian visitors who believe in the Resurrection go away again without being moved and elated as the Orthodox parishioners are. We wonder how that can be, when we are floating on the clouds of Paschal exaltation.

I think it may have to do with the fact that the visitors skipped the middle and went straight to the end. As Father Alexander Schmemann says in *Great Lent*, "The Church knows our inability to change rapidly, to go abruptly from one spiritual or mental state into another." Sadly, this happens even to Orthodox sometimes—members who are not in the habit of attending church every week without fail may sometimes show up for the Sunday of Orthodoxy and its pageantry, and then come to perhaps some of the Holy Week services, before attending Pascha itself. The sermon of John Chrystostom, read at the beginning of the Paschal Liturgy, welcomes them—"even those who have come at the eleventh hour"—but even so, they have cheated themselves of the Holy Spirit's powerful therapeutic program, designed to heal and mature us, to clothe us in the spiritual wedding garment suitable for the Feast.

And I think this need to go through the middle, not skip over it, is one reason the Church commemorates the power of the Cross at Mid-Lent. The Cross shows us the center of suffering, and the center of salvation. It is the meeting place of Death and Life, of God and Man.

The Cross was not the end for Jesus, it was only the middle—the gateway by which He passed from His earthly life, through death, to His glorious Resurrection. It is the same for us as we follow Him. Lent is given to us so that we may die to ourselves and be raised again gloriously with Christ our Savior.

This kind of thing happens in starkly dramatic terms in the middle of stories all the time. If you remember your *Star Wars*, you know what happened to Luke Skywalker in the middle of the story: he went into the dark place to face Darth Vader, only to find, when he had cut off the villain's head, that he had symbolically killed himself. But everyday life isn't so clearcut as a movie's story line, and the deaths to self that we experience are sometimes slow and laborious. That is why the Cross at the middle of Lent can help us focus again on God's plan for us.

The middle of our life is sometimes quite a muddle. We aren't sure where we are going any more—we have trouble with our health, our relationships, our career choices. We face doubt. We are distracted from the Cross by the everyday realities of balancing schedules, tending to families, persisting at our jobs.

Sometimes as we muddle along, we realize middles simply have to be endured. It can help, though, even just to remember that we are at the *middle*, that half the road is behind us already. And if we keep the Cross before us, we will remember that it is all about dying to self so that Christ can raise us up again. When we keep that truth firmly focused in our minds, it helps dispel the confusion, doubt, and weariness of mid-Lent, of mid-life.

The song we sing at Mid-Lent is a good one to remember all our life through: "Before Your Cross, we bow down in worship, O Master, and Your Holy Resurrection we glorify!"

Fourth Sunday of Lent
John Climacus

Picking a Fight

AS A WRITER OF FICTION, I spend a lot of time thinking about conflict. Stories go nowhere without it, but beginning writers often have misconceptions about what it is. They sometimes seem to have the idea—perhaps gleaned from the latest action movie, or even the evening news—that conflict has something to do with the sound of guns firing, or explosions bathing the screen in flame. But those things in themselves do not define conflict; they are only effects, or symptoms. Conflict is something that happens on the deepest levels of reality—not only in the human heart, but in the very fabric of this fallen universe.

Conflict begins when somebody wants something—and somebody else is standing in the way. The Book of Job gives us a glimpse behind the scenes of the cosmic drama at the very root of conflict, in the person of Satan. This name by which we know the ultimate evil principle is actually a title meaning "the Adversary." He is the one who appears on the opposite side of the court, fighting in the legal battle against the descendants of Adam. He wants something: primacy in God's creation. And we are in his way.

This war was begun long ago, and we have inherited it. When we are born into the human race, we are born into an ongoing conflict not of our making. But when we "put on Christ," when we receive the robe of light, whether as infants or as adult converts, we become "newly enlisted warriors of Christ" by virtue of baptism and chrismation. We are no longer bystanders in the cosmic war, but have declared our intention to take up arms against the Enemy. My husband likes to tell the newly received that their picture is now on "wanted" posters on the walls of every post office in Hell.

This is reality—not the daily grind of commuting or changing diapers or trying to pass your math test. Those are only a veil behind which a life-and-death struggle rages, every day.

There are many factors that can affect the outcome of a battle: charismatic leadership, clever strategy and tactics, even superior technology, to name only a few. History is full of stories where sheer numbers have been overcome by the courage of the less numerous side. But sometimes the inspiring leader is killed, the tactics that won the field prove inadequate to hold the ground gained, or the enemy upgrades his arms and equipment to surpass yours, so that after winning one battle, you find yourself in bewilderment losing the next.

Many different things may turn the tide of individual battles, but there is one thing that ultimately wins the war: persistence. As we sing in Matins this fourth Sunday in Lent, dedicated to the great spiritual warrior of the sixth century, St. John of the Ladder (Climacus), "With courage you have endured the assaults and wounds of the enemy; you are a pillar of steadfastness."

Perhaps you've heard the story of the monk who was asked, "What is it you do in that monastery all day long, anyway?" The monk replied, "We fall down and get up, fall down and get up . . ."

Lent is our chance to "get up" again every year. To be sure, we have daily opportunities. Just as St. John portrays in his spiritual treatise *The Ladder of Divine Ascent*, every choice we make either moves us a step toward victory, or gives the enemy an opening to strike at us. He employs guerrilla tactics, lying in wait while we waste time in front of the TV or computer, or as we rush headlong and harried through our overcommitted schedules. Great Lent, though, is the time when the Church goes on the offensive.

The regular fast days and fasting periods of the Church, but most especially Great Lent, are the times when the troops gather and synchronize their efforts, making rendezvous at the penitential services and individually fighting with their weapons of prayer, fasting, and almsgiving. The officers, the clergy, rally them with teachings from the Scriptures and the lives of mighty warriors who have gone before, like John of the Ladder, Gregory Palamas, and Mary of Egypt.

In the film *Braveheart,* William Wallace, the Scottish national hero, is trying desperately to unite and inspire all the scattered clans of Scotland. Without their unity and persistence, all of their countrymen will remain forever under the oppressive rule of the cruel King Edward and the English. Stung by English depredations and roused by Wallace's rhetoric, the Scots finally assemble for a pitched battle with the English. But as they restlessly await the signal to attack, they are betrayed by their own nobles, who go to a parlay with the enemy and prepare to accept bribes. If they leave the field now, the Scottish nobles and their English enemies both know, the clans will be demoralized and perhaps never be able to organize resistance again.

Wallace, waiting with the other commoners, sees what is happening, and prepares to advance upon the field.

"Where are you going?" his men call out.

Wallace grins wickedly in reply. "I'm goin' to pick a fight," he says.

That's what Lent is about. It is an all-out effort to advance against the enemy. We may have daily skirmishes with him at other times, but Lent is a pitched battle, a big push. In Lent, we do not retreat or hide from the enemy—we gather in force and prepare to engage him at *our* pleasure.

It would be easy to accept the bribes—surely we don't *really* have to fast? Nobody will miss us if we don't go to the Presanctified Liturgy, right? We pray enough, give enough money to the church throughout the year, don't we? Besides, we've done Lent before—it's just getting to be too much . . .

Make no mistake, we risk being hurt if we go to the battle. Very often, the Adversary will indeed just leave in peace those who offer him no threat. We wonder why sometimes bad things seem to happen to good people; in part, it is surely because, as we learn in the

Book of Job, the righteous stand in the way of Satan's plans, and provoke him to anger and jealousy with their obedience to God. But would we rather be like the Scottish nobles—content to live in our castles, at the expense of our fellow countrymen who are being harried by the enemy?

Think instead of picking a fight with the enemy this Lent. Wallace's persistence eventually won temporal freedom for his country. We are blessed to know the final outcome of the cosmic war, in which Christ wins the final victory over death and sin. How much more, then, should we be bold to go on the offensive this Lent?

"Our time is short," writes St. John Climacus. "Let us please the Lord as soldiers please the emperor; for at the end of the campaign we must give a good account of ourselves." The conflict will not go away because we are found missing in action. It is there, woven into the matrix of daily life; often we do not see how much ground we have already lost because we are used to sitting on the sidelines. The Lenten battle cry is sounded: *Repent!* and the standard of the Cross is raised. Who knows just how much might be accomplished in the spiritual conflict by any parish, any individual, who would rally to the fight, wholeheartedly risking their own comfort, persisting to the end?

Fifth Sunday of Lent
Mary of Egypt

Patron of Modesty

HOT SEXY BABES WANT TO MEET YOU!

Ever had one of these spams in your e-mail box?

If not, you've probably seen a bus-stop billboard ad for Buffalo jeans, with airbrushed male and female bodies posed provocatively, the too-tight jeans with the fly undone. Or caught a glimpse of the tabloid headlines as you went through the grocery checkout: [insert name of celebrity] Caught Cheating!

You can't go anywhere these days—not even to your e-mail box—without having unwanted words or images of a sexual nature thrust in your face. It's a challenge to get through even a single day without such distractions. I feel a little bad about adding to them here, in fact; but the flood is such that I don't think just ignoring it is an adequate response.

The sexual obsession of our culture is not really anything new; many ancient civilizations were infamous for their sexual depravity, as well as violence and idolatry, which all seem to be tied up together. What is new in our Information Age is the sheer volume of stuff that is laid on us from morning till night. You can give up TV and the Internet, you can homeschool the kids; you're still going to see the bus-stop ads on your way to church, or the tabloid headlines when you buy groceries.

What a relief to turn to Mary of Egypt, this fifth Sunday in Lent, to regain a little perspective. She didn't have the Internet or

Entertainment Tonight, but she did know all about the sex-saturated lifestyle, firsthand. In fact, in a city known for its debauchery, she was notorious for her outrageous behavior. The story of her life, as told to the Elder Zosima, makes clear that she did not take herself to be an unwilling victim; on the contrary, she admits shamefacedly how excessive were her passions, and how willingly she indulged them.

But something happened, as Mary continued acting the part of a prostitute, without even requiring pay, doing what she did because she was addicted. It seems the street life of Alexandria began to pale on her, and she began to look around for new excitement, settling finally on a ship that was departing for Jerusalem. The old hometown party was just not wild enough for her any more.

Wendy Shalit, in her landmark book *A Return to Modesty*, notes that the people who are products of an immodest culture eventually become jaded. When everyone is supposed to be having sex more or less indiscriminately, the spark of courtship between the sexes goes out. In contrast she cites a picture from the early 1900s, showing the thrill of innocent flirtation between modestly dressed young women and men. The boys knew they weren't gettin' any, and didn't expect to. Instead they were keeping an eye out for the right girl, the one they would marry.

How many young men did Mary of Egypt corrupt in her career, perverting them to think that this was the way women ought to behave, and this was how they should behave toward women? She can hardly bear to think of it, as she speaks to Zosima. She admits to seducing an entire shipful of men, men who were on a pilgrimage to the Feast of the Exaltation of the Cross in the holy places.

This holy shame did not happen all at once. We know the story of her repentance, brought about by her miraculous experience at the Church of the Resurrection in Jerusalem: An unseen hand refused her entrance to the church until she was forced to see herself as God saw her. Thereafter she fled into the desert. From pursuing the career of a whore who inveigled herself into a false intimacy with as many people as possible, Mary went instead to the ascetic life of a desert hermit, seeing no-one in any capacity for many years, until near the end of her life Divine Providence brought the priest Zosima to minister to her with the sacraments of the Church.

What a change in her self-presentation there was when the priest approached her: naked because her clothes had rotted away over the years, the woman who used to flaunt her sexual aggression like an ancient version of Madonna begged for a cloak to cover her shame.

Our world needs such a cloak to cover the daily shames that deface our media with lewd images and immoral philosophies of sex. Wendy Shalit proposes that a return to modesty, an attitude that respects the vulnerability of young women, will make all the difference. She notes that many young modern women are flocking to Jane Austen films, sighing over the portrayal of a gentler time, when men were expected to aspire to honorable behavior, and women had the power to say no to their sexual advances before they got anywhere near what would be considered first base today.

I think Ms. Shalit's book has analyzed the central problem of our society brilliantly. But there is more yet to be done, not least the presentation of a complementary view demonstrating how ill the sexual revolution has served men as well as women. We will not see the end of immodest ads for jeans until people stop buying them. We won't see the end of men's sexual presumption toward women until we stop treating such presumption as normal.

I am a little doubtful that the virtue of modesty can be got back into the box nowadays. As Orthodox Christians, we are already committed to living in a way that is not like the world's, and how much effect we have on the world around us is not so important as simply remaining faithful to Christ. Yet as St. Seraphim of Sarov tells us, if we acquire the Spirit of peace, thousands around us will be saved. If we follow Christ, our influence upon those we come in contact with will be out of all proportion.

That was certainly the case for Mary of Egypt. She may have corrupted thousands in her early life, but in her repentance she became a saint of the Church, and her reach extends now not to thousands but millions, as her story is celebrated throughout Orthodoxy on this Sunday in Lent every year. If the modesty movement ever wishes to adopt a patron saint, they could not do better than to choose Mary of Egypt.

March 25
Annunciation

Nothing Will Ever Be the Same

AS A KID I SPENT A LOT OF TIME with my nose stuck in a comic book. Nowadays the medium has become highly sophisticated (not to mention lucrative), featuring multi-layered characters, complex story lines, and artwork that dramatizes the human figure in action with a depth and power modernist art has forgotten could be possible. But back in the 1960s when I was devouring them at 12 cents a pop, comic books were simple: the heroes looked like ordinary people, but weren't. When duty called they put on their corny costumes and went off to battle evil and save the world with their super-powers.

The "secret identity" of the superhero is a motif that continues to fascinate us today, as speedily improving film technology brings comic book favorites like Spiderman and the X-Men to the big screen. We all want to think we could be something more than what we are. We all would like to think the rest of the world doesn't suspect that, deep down, we are anything but ordinary. We identify with the nerdy, neurotic teenager when he is bitten by a radioactive spider (in the updated movie version, it's genetically engineered instead) and ZAP!—he can crawl across ceilings and swat villains with his super-strength.

Reading the superheroes' "origin" stories was always one of the greatest pleasures for comic fans, because we could sense the promise of greatness from the first panel. We watched the bespectacled

Peter Parker hanging around the science exhibit, oblivious to the spider descending towards him on its web, just as the radioactive beam strikes it. A second later the dying arachnid bites the unsuspecting teenager, and we know what he doesn't yet—that from this moment on, Nothing Will Ever Be the Same.

Maybe one of the special appeals the superhero has for the preadolescents and adolescents who make up the bulk of comic book readership is this theme of the Big Change. They are after all on the threshold of their own Big Change—scary, exciting, and momentous.

And I guess that's part of why superheroes still appeal to people like me today. I cheerfully admit to never having entirely grown up yet. I am not much troubled by this because I think it is an intrinsically human state—and that only through the prism of an Orthodox worldview do we really begin to understand how our life is one long "becoming," a preparation for a final Big Change. It's only when we mistakenly think that we are already really grown up that we get ourselves into trouble.

The Feast of the Annunciation is a celebration of the ultimate, cosmic Big Change. The hero of this story too is a teenager, a girl from an apparently ordinary family who is soon revealed to be anything but ordinary.

Let's face it—when an angel appears and says "Hail!" the person hailed can't just go on living quietly the way she did before. Something life-shaking is about to happen—and when the angel Gabriel salutes the teenage girl who is to become Theotokos, we know it is not just life-changing but world-changing. Even if we approach the history of the world from a secular stance, we can pinpoint a great divide in world history here, at the place where Jesus comes into the world. Even to the outward eye, this Big Change is undeniable.

But like the superhero's friends and neighbors, the world is oblivious to the hidden reality. Where they see only the "Historical Jesus," a sort of ethical guru, the Church knows about the Person the Archangel Gabriel announces in the Gospel lesson for the feast (Luke 1:24–38), who "will be great . . . Son of the Highest . . . the Lord

God will give Him the throne of His father David. And He will reign over the House of Jacob forever, and of His Kingdom there will be no end."

In the Post-Reformation West, the figure of Mary Theotokos too fell into a pseudo-ordinariness. The angelic salutation to the girl who was to give birth to God Incarnate as "full of grace" and "blessed among women" has been virtually forgotten by Protestant Christians. Some years ago there was a "Jesus" video distributed for evangelistic purposes, which purported to reproduce faithfully and exactly the words of the Gospel of Luke, letting the New Testament speak for itself to a video-oriented generation; yet the "Hail Mary" was omitted. Conspicuous by its absence to Orthodox and Catholics, it was apparently never missed by the evangelicals involved in the video distribution project, despite their trumpeted devotion to biblical accuracy. They were simply too used to thinking of our Lord's mother as nobody special.

But of course she is somebody special. She has been overshadowed by the Power of the Most High. The Big Change ushered in by Gabriel's annunciation to her was more profound than that of any superhero's origin story. From the moment the angel appears, Mary realizes she is Not Ordinary; and as we read the Gospel account, so do we. For her and for the world, Nothing Will Ever Be the Same.

At the Feast of the Annunciation, as always, the Theotokos is the epitome of Christian obedience. The mistake of the Reformation, to make the mother of God-With-Us ordinary, has left Protestantism to the inevitable conclusion that so also are all of us ordinary. But in the Orthodox view, the Theotokos is the shining example of the extraordinary beings we are all called to be in Christ.

My all-time favorite comic-book quotation comes from the pages of Spiderman: "With great power comes great responsibility!" (If you wonder why comic book writing uses so many exclamation marks, it's because the writers want to be sure you know: these words are not ordinary!) The Scripture is clear that if we do not act on the teaching our Lord gives to us, it would be better for us never to have heard (2 Peter 2:21). The Theotokos' obedient response to Gabriel's message is as stark and simple as a snippet of comic-book dialogue: "Behold the handmaiden of the Lord!"

That's our line too. But we must speak it in the full knowledge that anyone who joins the service of the Son of the Highest will no longer be ordinary. From the moment we become His, Nothing Will Ever Be the Same.

Part VI

The Lord's Last Road—Holy Week

Lazarus Saturday

The Power of Tears

"JESUS WEPT."

I can remember Sunday School quizzes identifying this statement from the Gospel for Lazarus Saturday as the shortest verse in the Bible (John 11:35). But of course the original Greek manuscripts had no verses marked; the words were just there. And this simple statement, "Jesus wept," is much more than a curiosity.

Tears have tremendous power in our human experience. Our modern Western culture has not much appreciation for tears; it tends to regard them as something to be suppressed by adults, and especially by men. Yet many a big, tough man will admit that while he can abide any sort of pain or suffering, he will dissolve at once into helplessness when faced with a woman's tears. Perhaps that is exactly why our society fears and denigrates tears—because of this amazing power they have over those who seem impervious to all other attempts to entreat them.

Tears have many meanings. They may represent contrition and a heart swelling with overflowing love, as with the woman anointing our Lord's feet, washing them with her tears (Luke 7:38). Or they may signal an epiphany for the person who sheds them, as we often see at the climax of some dramatic film or play, when all the pressures of the narrative become too much for the main character, who may then make a pivotal speech on the theme of the story. As in the old fairy tale, *Rapunzel*, the healing of blindness often follows tears.

But of all the many reasons for weeping, perhaps it is mourning that comes most quickly to mind when we think of tears. Even if we think we have them tamped down at one of our starchy, artificial North American funerals, the tears are there, even if unshed.

The power of mourning is vividly illustrated in the old Norse myth of the god Baldur, the brightest, purest, and most beautiful of the gods. All his fellow gods loved him and feared for his safety, and therefore extracted a promise from all created things to refrain from hurting the beautiful god, thus rendering him invulnerable. But when the treachery of the jealous, Satan-like god Loki finds a way to circumvent this prohibition, the gods make an agreement with the queen of the dead to return Baldur to life. They have only to ensure that every living being weeps for him.

Wouldn't this be a great demonstration of the power of tears, to have them overcome death? But ah, tears have their limitations—there is a single being who refuses to weep for Baldur: a lone witch-woman who is doubtless the malicious Loki in disguise—and so the land of the dead holds Baldur fast forever.

In the folklore tradition that persisted long after Europeans had ceased to worship the Northern Gods like Loki and Baldur, it is only witches who do not weep. Their deal with the devil has stolen something essential in their humanity, so that they can be so cold as never to weep, and most especially cold toward their fellow creatures. How chilling, then, that our post-Christian culture should now look on tears as a sign of weakness or immaturity, when in fact they are simply the badge of humanity.

The Lazarus Saturday services confirm this view of tears. The hymns and verses recount the weeping of Jesus at his friend Lazarus's tomb with tenderness but not maudlin sentiment, calling His tears not only "proof of heartfelt love" (Compline, Canticle 7) but something much more profound, singing to Christ that "Thou hast truly taken flesh at Thine Incarnation, and that being God by nature Thou hast become by nature a man like us. . . . Thou hast made the tears of Martha and Mary to cease, O Lord and Savior, by raising Lazarus from the dead."

Tears, and most especially the tears of mourning for the beloved departed, are a signal characteristic of the essential human nature. But unlike the Norse myth, the liturgical texts do not see these tears of Jesus as the power that could bring someone back from the dead. Instead it is His breath, His voice, His words that call Lazarus back from Hades where the dead dwell. The third canticle of Compline gives words to Hades itself, which cries out, "Woe is me! Now I am destroyed utterly . . . the man from Nazareth has shaken the lower world, and cutting open my belly He has called a lifeless corpse and raised it up."

People who weep at the death of a loved one often reason, "I'm not weeping for them, I'm weeping for myself." They believe, if they are Christians at least, that the departed is in a better place, and they who remain behind in mourning weep because they will miss the loved one, at least until they are reunited. But this is not at all why Jesus wept, for He knew He was about to bring Lazarus back into the land of the living once more. While Mary and Martha spoke to Him tearfully of how Lazarus would surely have lived, if only their Master had gotten there sooner, Jesus Himself claimed to His Apostles, "I am glad for your sakes that I was not there, that you may believe."

He knew the happy ending already when He heard of Lazarus's illness. Did He then weep merely *pro forma*? Because it was expected of Him, just to prove He was indeed a friend of the departed, even though He had deliberately delayed His coming, effectively allowing Lazarus to die? The services of Lazarus Saturday do not entertain any such thought. They say He wept precisely because He did love Lazarus, as He loves each one of us.

He wept as we ourselves might weep at seeing a loved one taken captive and held in some dreadful place, like a hostage held by terrorists. Even we do not weep only for ourselves in such a case, for missing the loved one, but also for them in their suffering.

We find it hard to weep for people we do not know. We can hear of thousands of children being orphaned daily by AIDS or floods or earthquakes in far-off places, and never weep for them. Show us television pictures of individual orphans, eyes gazing imploringly at the camera and with flies landing on their unkempt heads, and perhaps we may be moved to emotion, even tears, hope-fully to help them. If we see someone we already know and love suffering right in front of us, it is more likely still that we may cry for them.

There is the secret of Our Lord's weeping which proves Him both human and divine at once—He wept for Lazarus because He knew and loved Him. And because He knows and loves each of us, members of His errant flock, He condescended to do this miracle of resurrection of the man four days dead, so that we too may believe.

Palm Sunday
Our Lord's Triumphal Entry into Jerusalem

Sacred Child's Play

BEING CHILDLIKE COMES HARD in this world. There is such a push to turn children, at ever younger ages, into miniature adults—or, rather, into tiny adolescents, bedeviled by adult choices and problems, without yet having the skills and wisdom to deal with them.

You know what I'm talking about. JonBenet Ramsey. Littleton, Colorado. Twelve-year-olds throwing rocks at soldiers in the Middle East. Girls and boys alike sold into prostitution in Southeast Asia. Sex and violence and long-lost innocence.

In a world where children scarcely have a childhood, it is no wonder adults have trouble recapturing the childlike spirit without which we cannot enter the Kingdom of Heaven (Mark 10:15). After a prolonged irresponsible adolescence in our Western society, many people seem to settle down in their thirties to a grimly responsible adulthood, cramming all the waking hours with work, and determinedly driving their own children through a never-ending series of extracurricular sports, music lessons, and the like.

Disney's *Fantasia 2000* brilliantly illustrates the loss of—and our desperate need for—a childlike spirit of play. In the Gershwin "Rhapsody in Blue" sequence, we follow several characters and their longings through a hectic day in Depression-era New York. One of them, a curly-headed little girl, is fobbed off on a nanny by her stylishly dressed parents. The nanny propels the child from one activity to another—voice lessons, piano lessons, swimming, dance class—the frantic pace of each scene ratcheting higher as the music crescendos.

In another story line, a childlike little man trails his prim socialite wife and her lap dog on an outing to the pet supply shop. Toys, in the view of the wife, are not actually to be played with, as the little man attempts to do, but simply to be amassed and paid for.

At one point in the musical-animation sequence, the individual characters all gaze longingly at the skaters on a rink, daydreaming about the joy and freedom that are lacking in their driven lives. The miserable child longs for her parents to take her skating and lift her between them, swinging over the surface of the ice; and the constrained little man fantasizes about barreling down the length of the rink and leaping into the air with the birds for the sheer fun of it. A reluctant construction worker eagerly anticipates performing as a drummer at talent night, and an unemployed man's dream of securing a job transfigures the very idea of work itself into exuberant play.

One often hears that "Christmas is really for the children," as if it were improper for adults to enjoy feasting, exchanging gifts, music and decorations. But the Church has never designated her feasts "especially" for one group or another—this feast for mothers, that for fathers, another for children. The weekly feast of Eucharist on the Lord's Day in the Orthodox Church is served "on behalf of all and for all," and communion offered to every member of the baptized fellowship, even to the babes in arms.

There is, however, one feast in the Calendar with an intimate connection to the joy of childhood: Palm Sunday, when the children led the procession of our Lord's triumphal entry into Jerusalem. Waving palm branches and shouting exultant hosannas, they could not be silent, or "the stones would immediately cry out" (Luke 19:40).

It seems certain that the younger ones, at least, had no idea what the ruckus was all about. The adults understood that the land was churning with political unrest; they hoped that Jesus would be the leader to throw off the Roman yoke. They must have felt His arrival in Jerusalem bore all the weight of history in the making, and their excitement could not have been unmixed with apprehension.

The children, however, knew only the thrill of a big public event. They didn't think about what they were doing or why. It was simply fun to wave the palms and shout "Hosannna!" for the Man on the donkey.

Sometimes that's all we need, too—to seize the opportunities that come our way to do something unexpected, with the joyful abandon of children. Why not build a gingerbread house—even if there are no children in your household? Sing a silly song—loudly! Or try lying down in the snow and making a snow angel.

Why, I even know one nun (who perhaps had best remain nameless) who kicked up her heels and gave a gathering of friends a brief demonstration of the Highland fling she had learned long ago in childhood!

Adults who learn not to resist such impulses to holy child's play are as likely as the children of Palm Sunday to burst into spontaneous cries of "Hosanna!" Like the little man in the movie, a playful spirit turns our hearts upward. Only thus childlike will we enter the Kingdom of Heaven.

The Bridegroom Services of Holy Week

Jilted at the Altar

EVERYBODY LOVES A WEDDING. Okay, maybe we don't love the boring speeches or the embarrassing relatives that we have to put up with at the reception, but face it, nobody can resist a blushing bride decked out in white lace and fragrant flowers.

"...when you are married, you go back to church dressed up like you never were before in all your days," writes Virginia Cary Hudson, aged 10, circa 1904, in her collection of unintentionally hilarious essays, *O Ye Jigs and Juleps!* "Somebody sings 'O Promise Me' and your sweetheart is waiting up by the preacher, if," young Virginia concludes, "he doesn't forget to come...."

Jilted at the altar! This horrible thought has a place in modern mythology that looms large in the imagination and provides terrific fodder for sitcoms, though in real life it is rare enough. A kind of reverse Cinderella story, in which the gorgeously gowned princess-for-a-day is struck down from her glittering pedestal to the humiliation of the ash-heap.

When I was in high school, *jilted at the altar* was the whispered explanation for one thirtyish, ill-tempered woman teacher who displayed a notable bias against her male students, and insisted on being called *Ms.* in those days when political correctness had not yet taken hold. We accepted the tale because we all acknowledged that such an ultimate rejection was certainly enough to sour a person for a lifetime.

It's a popular myth still in this twenty-first century. As one character says with a rueful shake of her head in Connie Willis's comic novel about fads and trends, *Bellwether*, "So many guys have intimacy issues these days."

We have no trouble envisioning the girl in white having her heart very publicly broken by a callous male. The aftermath of the sexual revolution has long ago shattered the last remnants of romanticism in our culture. With sex ostensibly free and easy, and commitment no longer a foregone conclusion, it's harder than ever to get a guy up the aisle. In such a social atmosphere, the *jilted at the altar* motif has only increased in mythic power, and the would-be bride so rejected seems a more pitiful figure than ever before. It is the stuff of nightmares, as haunting and horrifying as any Hallowe'en monster.

Living in such a society, it's hard for us to identify with the parable of the wise and foolish bridesmaids which holds an important place in the services early in Holy Week (Matthew 25:1–13). Having thrown off the yoke of male-driven stereotypes, and along with it male protection, postmodern feminist rhetoric too often casts women as victims. Men in turn are demonized as aggressors, condemned and reviled as testosterone-driven animals. Weddings in our world are thrilling and exciting, a glimpse of a longed-for fairy tale; but they lack the seal of permanence in a culture that disdains chastity and is addicted to divorce.

So we come to view our Lord's story about a wedding from the point of view of some of the participants, not the couple themselves, but the bride's young unmarried friends. Even more than today, a wedding was very much a community event, and those most excited by the pageantry were those who might themselves hope to wear the bridal veil sometime in the near future.

The first-century marriage was a contract between families, in two parts—the betrothal, and the later acceptance of the bride into the groom's house. This latter ceremony, at night, consisted in the bridegroom's arrival with his torch-bearing entourage at the bride's home, there to carry her off to his own home, where the guests would join in the well-wishing and merry-making long into the night.

The maidens in the parable are part of this entourage, waiting to be picked up along the way by the rest of the procession. With no precise time-keeping instruments, they could only know the bridegroom would come to collect them well after dark. Their lamps or torches would have fuel only for a few hours at most, and the wise maidens had brought along additional supplies. The foolish ones, failing to plan ahead, must go out to find a vendor of oil; thus missing the bridegroom's arrival, they are afterward denied entry to the wedding feast.

Imagine missing a wedding! For those ancient people, it may have been still more unthinkable than for us. A wedding was the social event of the year—and in those days when they might have to travel from miles around, it was for the young friends and relatives of the bride and groom a chance to themselves see and be seen by prospective mates and their families. To run out of oil was not only a careless oversight leading to disappointment, it was a profound embarrassment that would give the girl an instant reputation as a poor housekeeper. Her own marriage prospects would plummet after such an incident.

In a world longing for love and certainty, we think of being jilted at the altar as the ultimate tragedy. To have the fairy-tale ending within our grasp, only to have it snatched away by a lover who proves to be false, seems unthinkable. But the Bridegroom Matins services of Holy Week turn that expectation on its head. The Heavenly Bridegroom is trustworthy, His advent certain. It is we who are careless and loveless, failing to provide the one small thing needful. Like silly adolescents who never think ahead, we leave it to the last minute to "prepare our lamps with the virtues and right faith," as one of the hymns exhorts us to do.

Holy Thursday

The Villain of the Piece

ACTORS OFTEN SAY it is "fun" to play the villain, and some writers claim to find evil characters more "interesting" to write than good ones. I'm not sure I've ever quite understood this myself, because good characters are the ones I find endlessly fascinating. It is true that goodness is quite difficult to portray fictionally. We don't often meet with real goodness in everyday life; and fiction, to capture and hold the attention of readers, actually needs to be *more* believable than real life. There are, however, some great good characters in the history of literature, such as Alyosha in *The Brothers Karamazov*, or Ender Wiggin in *Ender's Game*, characters luminous with joy, expansive generosity, childlike innocence, or self-sacrificing nobility.

Unless we are closely acquainted with people who routinely put their lives on the line for others, however, we don't so easily recognize goodness in the people we meet in our daily lives. They are too full of flaws, neuroses, annoying quirks. They are too much like ourselves, though we don't usually care to stop and think about that much.

On the other hand, we see villains on the nightly news all the time, even if we don't personally meet up with them. The pimps, the drug dealers, the serial killers. The terrorists. As each new horror unfolds on the small screen, accompanied by the newscaster's even-voiced commentary, we ask in astonishment, "How could anybody do such a thing?" We are repeatedly shocked, even in our jaded culture, at the actions of people who, we assume, must be nothing at all like us.

When it comes to movies or books, an effective villain is often one we "love to hate." This is because his actions are so outrageous, he makes us feel righteous by comparison, even—or especially—if he may be in other ways amusing or admirable. We wholeheartedly long for the bad guy to get what he deserves, and are not often disappointed.

As any actor will tell you, it's all in the motivation. The truth is, in real life the dividing line between good and evil may be blindingly obvious to an outside observer; but within the murky confines of the human soul it is often elusive. Souls are not often sold whole, but more often one small piece at a time, until, without knowing it, the person has lost it all. Like the foolish maidens remembered in the Bridegroom services of Holy Week, he has let the oil in his lamp run out, and has fallen into darkness (Matthew 25·8).

John LeCarré's realistic espionage novels, shorn of the glamour and adventure of James Bond and his ilk, often portray this downward spiral of the character of the spy. For a man whose whole way of life is betrayal, it becomes hard to know which side he is on, or whether in fact he has any ultimate loyalties.

But sometimes the person realizes he has one last chance, one final moment of truth. A chance to say a final "No" to the Dark Side.

One of my favorite fictional portrayals of such a pivotal moment appears in Lois McMaster Bujold's science fiction novel *Memory*. As in a LeCarré story, the hero works undercover, in this case for an interplanetary empire. Miles Vorkosigan serves his liege emperor and his home planet willingly, not for money. There is, however, considerable ego invested in his alternate identity. When he becomes medically unfit, endangering the life of someone he was supposed to rescue, he is so desperate to continue living this other identity that he falsifies a report, which is then found out, getting him cashiered from the service.

Miles is purposeless and suicidally depressed until he is needed to investigate an attack on his former superior. And as the various red herrings appear and disappear, the new boss offers him his old job, his old identity back . . . *if* he will wind up the investigation now, while only one suspect is in view. A suspect Miles knows to be innocent.

Miles declines to play Judas . . . but not without a struggle. He even entertains the possibility that the man he is asked to betray might be guilty after all. As he paces and pounds on the floor, trying to think what to choose, his family comes upstairs to inquire just what he is doing. "Just . . . wrestling with temptation," he says. To the amused query, "Who's winning?" he makes the quite serious reply, "I think . . . I'm going for the best two falls out of three."

The line between good and evil, friend and betrayer, is sometimes that close. The difficulty is to see it—and even then, temptation may win the best two of three falls after all.

We aren't asked, in the services of Holy Week, to fully understand the motives of Judas in his betrayal of Jesus, nor do we trace his whole downward spiral from chosen apostle to traitor. The liturgical poetry does, however, reiterate the Gospel testimony that he was regularly embezzling money from the common purse (John 12:6). This appears to have been common knowledge among the Twelve, and yet they could do nothing about it as Jesus was content to let Judas remain with the band, allowing wheat and tares to grow together (Matthew 13:30). Judas, it appears, was to be given his chance at two out of three falls in the wrestling match with temptation. If his motivation perhaps began with something as simple as easy money, he spiraled downward as he became willing not just to pilfer from the Man he called Master, but to actually betray Him to His enemies.

We know where this ended: the consequences spun out of control, and Judas hanged himself, "gaining nothing from his regrets," against which the service of Holy Friday Matins (commonly celebrated Thursday evening) warns us (Antiphon IV).

How could he have done it? Surely we couldn't do such a thing, could we? The hymns for Holy Thursday Matins speak with their characteristic sense of paradox and irony of how Judas sold the One "above all price" for a finite amount of coin. Anyone can see from outside that it was a bad bargain, that the line between good and evil was clearly drawn. But Judas was not seeing clearly. ("When your eye is good, your whole body also is full of light. But when *your* eye is bad, your body also *is* full of darkness" Luke 11:34.)

In *Memory*, Miles Vorkosigan's friends, who know his desperate attachment to his old Covert Ops identity, are surprised to find out he has won the battle with temptation and refused the bribe. When they ask why, he says, "Some prices are just too high, no matter how much you may want the prize. The one thing you can't trade for your heart's desire is your heart."

We may never know the whole of what impelled Judas to become "the villain of the piece" through the choices he made, any more than we know what motivates the terrorists and criminals on the evening news. What we do know is that if Jesus had been at the center of Judas's heart, no other heart's desire could have offered sufficient temptation for such a betrayal. It might have been as close as two falls out of three, but at the end of the day he would have remained squarely on the side of good.

From the Presanctified Liturgy of Holy Thursday we take this communion hymn, which has struck such a chord with the faithful that we now sing it regularly at liturgies throughout the year:

"Of Your mystical supper, O Son of God, accept me today as a communicant. For I will not speak of Your mystery to Your enemies, neither like Judas will I give You a kiss, but like the thief will I confess you: Remember me, O Lord, in Your kingdom."

Holy Friday

Slow-Motion Suffering

WHEN YOU INVITE PEOPLE TO CHURCH, you don't want them to suffer. But I'm afraid that's just what happened when some curious friends of ours from a Western liturgical church came to our Orthodox service on the evening of Holy Thursday. Their Holy Week happened not to coincide with ours that year, and they thought they would check out how the other half lives. It was, I guess, the worst possible service they could have chosen for their first visit to an Orthodox church. My husband had given them a woefully inadequate estimate of the length of this service, and at last, two-thirds of the way through the evening, they had to take their wilting children and depart.

What is this service, and why is it so lengthy? I got a pretty impressive double-take from another non-Orthodox friend when I said something about the service of "the Twelve Gospels." *Er, aren't there just four?* Right, we Orthodox aren't quite as nutty as all that—it's just shorthand for "twelve Gospel lessons," readings from the words of Matthew, Mark, Luke, and John. In the Holy Friday Matins (commonly celebrated on Thursday evening), we turn our attention to the inspired writings of the four Evangelists on the Passion of our Lord, His suffering to redeem us on the Cross.

Time flies when you're having fun, they say. But if you have ever been in pain, you know the seconds crawl by in slow motion when you are suffering, so that all you can think is, *Will this never end?* Now, it isn't that we Orthodox think that since Jesus suffered, we should suffer too, and therefore we feel obliged to have the most grueling, depressing, dragged-out service possible. Put like that, it sounds pretty silly—and so it should, for such a view of suffering is heretical.

At this most solemn commemoration of the Church year, the story of the first Holy Friday is incorporated into the Matins service. But of such import are the events of this day, the Church has found it inadequate to simply read a short lesson on our Lord's Crucifixion and then perhaps have a homily upon it. Instead, we are invited to enter deeply into this mystery of the suffering of God Incarnate, who yet does not suffer. We listen patiently, candles alight in our hands, to everything the Gospel writers put down about the terrible events that began at Gethsemane, passed to Pilate's judgment hall and then through the streets of Jerusalem to Calvary, and ended at last in a borrowed tomb.

It is instructive to look at the lessons as they appear in *The Lenten Triodion*. Unlike in whatever Bible you may have at home on the bedside table or in the icon corner, the text is not broken up into little bite-sized verses. And the first of these twelve readings (John 13:31—18:1) has almost no action, but instead consists of a long discourse our Lord gave to His Apostles when they came out from their last Passover together, moving toward the garden where He would pray to have this cup of agony taken away from Him. That terrible night, the Apostles spent a lot of time—as they so often did—just listening to what their Master had to say to them.

There's no shame, of course, if we find it a challenge to keep our attention focused during this service—the Apostles themselves found it too much to stay awake all through the night while Jesus prayed in Gethsemane. But the Church in her wisdom thinks it best in her liturgical services not to diminish the full reality of that dreadful time. Instead she offers us everything available, to help us to begin to realize the enormous and truly awesome nature of what Christ did for us.

In a short article like this, I don't think I can even begin to express the terrible wonder of these events that changed the nature of reality forever. A great poet might do so—for instance, the anonymous poet who wrote the Old English poem, "The Dream of the Rood," *rood* being an archaic word for cross. This writer makes the Cross itself speak, telling the story of how "Almighty God ungirded Him / eager to mount the gallows / unafraid in the sight of many; / He would set free mankind" (trans. Michael Alexander). This poet conveyed brilliantly in the forms of his day the "sublime paradoxes of the Crucifixion" (Cassidy & Ringler, *Bright's Old English Grammar and Reader*).

But even this unnamed genius did not compose his masterpiece in isolation; ultimately his poem is based on the Passion account of Matthew 27, and the Passiontide liturgical services of his own time and place.

"The Dream of the Rood" takes the form of a vision which comes to the poet in the deep midnight, while all the world sleeps. Compared to the service of the Twelve Gospels, it is a fleeting thing, but the rhythmic verses capture our attention with a feeling of time-lessness, as the poet describes how the appearance of the Cross changes repeatedly before his gaze, "again clad in gold / or again slicked with sweat, / spangled with spilling blood."

Have you ever watched the climax of an action movie, and seen how the director chose to put some piece of pivotal action into slow motion? It is because, as things reach a crux like this, they become too complex and intense for our ordinary human senses to follow. And more than just enabling us to follow the chronology of events, a slow-motion sequence gives us the chance to experience the emo-tional impact of a climax that otherwise might be over too quickly for us to apprehend.

This begins to tell us why the Passion Gospels service moves by so slowly, revealing the final events of our Lord's earthly life in great detail. As we near the dark end of Holy Week, the many strands of the story are coming together in a dreadful paroxysm of betrayal, humiliation, and pain. We need to slow down and watch the Pas-sion events unfold, or they will be gone too quickly for us to take them to heart, swallowed up in the coming glory of the Resurrec-tion. We long for that Resurrection, but we dare not hurry ahead to it before time. The way for us is *per crucis ad lucis,* through the Cross to the light, through the slow motion of suffering with Christ to the sudden triumph of the New Day.

Holy Saturday
Shroud Procession

Untidy Death

THE RECENT DISCOVERY IN GEORGIA of a crematorium fraud has brought the reality of death and decay to TV screens in a way that most people have succeeded in eliminating from their consciousness entirely. The funeral industry has sanitized death and hidden its dreadful ravages upon the human body. Increasingly at non-Orthodox "funerals," cremation has become trendy. There is no body present at the service to receive the final kiss, as it is in the Orthodox practice. The deceased is instead whisked away from home or hospital as quickly as possible, and some of the mourners will never even have the chance to see the reality of the person in death, not even in the embalmed and cosmetically arranged form that is the usual alternative to cremation these days.

Behind the scenes, the crematorium staff is entrusted with disposing of the dead by loading them into a high-temperature oven. What the family gets back is a tidy little urn of ashes, which they often scatter in some spot the deceased had been fond of in life. No decay, no unpleasantness, nothing to make anyone want to hold their nostrils closed. No reminder of the profound change we must all undergo when we depart this life.

From this illusion of sanitized death, the victims of the Georgia crematorium fraud received a most rude awakening. The remains of their loved ones were not returned to them as they had thought, in antiseptic and decorative packages, but dumped unceremoniously along with others in various spots on the crematorium property. It may take years and considerable technological power for those remains to be sorted out before they can be properly disposed of, granting the mourners some kind of relief from their distress.

The world of first-century Judaism was far from ever being under the illusion that death is something that can be dealt with neatly. Unlike many of the pagan cultures surrounding them from earliest times, ancient Israel did not practice cremation of the dead; and the Church too kept what archaeologists call "inhumation" instead of burning as their standard burial practice, even in the face of stubborn resistance from the pagan peoples they evangelized in the post-Roman period. Cremation, for Orthodox, has remained an exceptional practice, permitted only if required by the state, or in extreme situations, such as an epidemic.

First-century burial practices had some challenges to meet: if you were not going to burn a dead body, it was necessary to take steps, in the hot climate, to minimize any contagion and stench. They borrowed a leaf from the book of the Egyptians and wrapped the corpse in linen, anointing it with aromatic oils and spices; but without taking the Egyptian-style extensive steps toward mummification, aimed at preserving the body for an imagined afterlife. The Jews instead left the final fate of the body to God, believing, as Martha says after Lazarus' death (John 11:24), in a general resurrection of the dead at the end of the world.

We modern Orthodox need to remind ourselves of this context when we come to the celebration of the quintessential funerary service, the procession of our Lord's shroud on the night between Holy Friday and Holy Saturday. Martha and Mary, as we have seen only a week earlier in the story of Christ raising Lazarus from the tomb, were well acquainted with the horror of death. Martha hesitated to obey the Lord when He asked to have her brother's tomb opened four days after his death. With characteristic bluntness, she objected, "Lord, by now he stinks!"

But in the end, Christ raised Lazarus from the dead. What then must Martha have thought when she saw the Master Himself go down to the enemy she had already seen Him defeat once? What did His mother and disciples think?

The services of the Shroud offer poetic expressions of what they all must have felt that dark day; the style is far removed from our restrained modern approach to death and mourning, and indeed quite a shock to Western sensibilities. These words are sung of the Virgin in the Vespers of Holy Friday as she beholds her Son and Lord disfigured by the tortures and violent death of the crucifixion: "She mourned within herself and was sorely pierced in her heart. She groaned in agony from the depth of her soul. Exhausted from tearing her hair and cheeks and beating her breast, she cried out lamenting . . . 'Where is the beauty of Thy form, O my Son?' "

No neatly packaged ashes for these mourners; they watched their Beloved die, His complexion drained to paleness from blood loss, His features bruised and battered by the soldiers' abuse. In the tender words of the Aposticha for this day, we hear how Joseph of Arimathea stepped forward to offer burial for this convicted criminal whom he adored as Master: "Joseph of Arimathea took Thee down from the tree, the Life of All, cold in death. Bathing Thee with sweet and costly myrrh, he gently covered Thee with finest linen, and with sorrow and tender love in his heart, he embraced Thy most pure body . . ."

At the end of this service, the "Shroud" (also known as the *epitaphion* or *plaschonitsa*) is carried to the center of the church. This icon depicting our Lord's removal from the Cross is then laid on a bier, where it is adorned with flowers and venerated by the faithful.

Martha said it quite plainly: death stinks. Unless we get hold of this reality, we cannot begin to grasp the profundity of mourning felt by our Lord's followers on that terrible day, nor the immensity of His triumph on the third day. They could not fully understand beforehand that the dreadful inevitability that awaits all living things—being turned into food for worms—would find its universal power stymied by Him.

It is fitting that our response to the remembrance of the awesome events of Holy Friday is a simple one. We do not try to explain, soften, or tidy up the devastation of death; instead, in the

Matins service of Holy Saturday, we take up the Shroud and bear it around the church in a solemn funeral procession. No consolation is adequate as we mourn the Death of the Life of All. Instead we fall back on the minor-key funeral ode with its desperate plea, "Holy God, Holy Mighty, Holy Immortal, have mercy on us."

For now, it's as if we haven't the heart to hope in the face of this most untidy death. But the end of the Matins service gives the smallest hint of triumph to come, as we sing the hymn about Joseph begging the body of our Lord from Pilate. In the mournful, gentle tone we repeat the refrain, "We worship Thy Passion, O Christ!" and conclude with the grace note, "and Thy Holy Resurrection."

Part VII

Pascha, the Feast of Feasts

Part VIII

Finding the Lessons Learned

Paschal Matins Procession

Lighting One Another's Candles

paschal procession
light passing from hand to hand
flames against the wind

FEW THINGS EXEMPLIFY the Christian community like the
Paschal procession, three times round the church at midnight. On a
busy road, we draw stares from weekend partygoers passing in their
cars. The wind puffs out some of our candles; but no-one is lost, for
we have gathered together in the darkness and shared our illumination, relighting each other's candles amid joyous laughter.

The cross is at the head of our column, and praise is in our
mouths.

How easy it is, on Pascha night, with our spirits keyed up
from weeks of Lenten labor, anticipating the Feast of Feasts—the
transfigured nave of the church decked in a blaze of white flowers;
the glorious greetings of "Christ is Risen!" at the Paschal communion; the community meal lavish with ham, cheese, paschal breads,
chocolate.

"Better to light one candle, than to curse the dark," goes the
proverb. Better yet, let many candles be lit, and relit if they falter,
from the flames of their fellows.

Easy, on Pascha night. But even throughout the year, we need
to keep our light shining, and share it with our fellow-Christians.
Throughout the year, the darkness and wind take many forms.

A business collapses. A man betrays his wife. An infant dies. How to relight the candles of the brothers and sisters assaulted by these violent gusts of wind?

We do well to remember, first, that the light we bear is not our own. We are only sharers of something we have received. We are beggars telling other hungry folk where we have found food. Thrust your candle in their faces too suddenly, and you may blind and startle them into retreat.

However, difficult as it may be to accept, even with the offer held out gently, you cannot relight someone else's candle without their cooperation. You can stand before them with your light held steady, but they can still hide their own candle behind their back, refusing to take their place once more in the shining procession.

On Pascha night that would seem silly—people laugh at the wind, then, and march on around the church, scarcely willing to pause long enough to brace their hands to recapture the flames offered by their neighbors. But somehow the storms of daily life in ordinary time seem to sweep some of us off the path. It happens most often when we feel ourselves alone, without fellow-marchers to relight our candles.

This is one reason why it is not merely a duty, but essential to our Christian life not only to attend services, but to actively participate in the ongoing life of our local parish—to keep circling the church, so to speak. A coal on the hearth keeps on burning, but if it gets dislodged and rolls away from the other coals on the fire, it soon fizzles. And the loss of even one coal makes the hearth-fire burn less brightly. It's a kind of false humility to assume one has nothing to offer or won't be missed at the local parish.

Conversely, we must never think that just because we go to a church service, enjoy the music, pray our prayers, receive communion, that we are therefore leading a pious life. There are even some otherwise devout folks who make a practice of "church-hopping." I'm not referring here to those who may find themselves in an irregular parish situation because of changes in health, difficult family situations, irregular job hours, or seasonal residence changes due to work or school. The people I am concerned about are those who leave parish after parish when they have a falling-out with the clergy or other members; or, perhaps even worse, those who simply make a habit of perennially "visiting" all the parishes in the area, so that they never seem to be real members of any one parish.

People in such situations think they have their own little candle burning; but if they are suddenly taken ill, which congregation will realize they are missing from the procession of parish life? And how will they ever know if they themselves might have been just the person needed to relight the candle of those other members they never got to know?

Perhaps you remember that camp song, "This little light of mine," which refers to the Gospel lesson about not hiding one's light under a bushel. There is only one Light, Christ (John 8:12), from whom all our little candles are lit. But He chooses to use our fellow Christians to pass that light along to us; and each of us in turn must live solely to share that light with others, first with the fellowship of light, the Church, and then with the world beyond.

There are many candles in our life, just as there are many in the church temple, in the altar and before the various icons. We can share our light in many ways—visiting the sick, driving others to church, teaching in church school, offering a listening ear to the troubled.

But all these things can only be done if we first simply keep on processing around the church—just continually being with the people God has appointed our fellow-marchers at our local parish. Don't hurry off to lunch before the after-church coffee is over; make an effort to invite fellow parishioners to your home, or to attend the women's group. You will then find there is somebody there to relight your candle when it blows out; and, perhaps even more blessed, you may be there to relight theirs.

Pascha

This Is the Day of Resurrection

A WRITER OF MY ACQUAINTANCE once called me up to say he was working on a novel about religion in the future, and for various reasons needed some information about Orthodoxy. Since his own Christian background was ancient history to him, he had a hard time knowing even where to begin asking questions. After a few stabs in the dark (*Is there an intercessory tradition of saints? Is it true you can look at icons as "windows to heaven"?*) he asked me to talk about something that was particularly meaningful to me in my Orthodox life.

I took a deep breath and was off and running before I knew it. "The liturgical year," I said. The cycle of feasts and fasts constantly reinforces and makes real the dogmas of the Church. The twelve major feasts help us relive our Lord's life. The waxing and waning seasons of Advent, Christmas, Lent, Pascha, Pentecost, all train us in the life rhythms of the salvation history that transcends our mortal time and space.

Even each day of the week has its special dedication, I enthused to my colleague on the other end of the phone. Sunday, for example, celebrates the Resurrection, as can be seen from the Scripture readings and hymns in Matins. "We Orthodox never lose sight of the Resurrection," I said.

"And what does the Resurrection mean to you, then?" my friend asked.

That one was hard to answer, because the answer is so large.

Orthodox Christianity is an historical religion; we do not live our lives based on myths, however powerful and beautiful. Or perhaps I should say we follow the True Myth, the Story that is bigger than our here and now, and yet has in fact invaded the here and now of human history. We believe that the man called Jesus was none other than God Incarnate, second Person of the Holy Trinity; and we believe He rose from the dead, physically and spiritually—He was not merely resuscitated, like a cardiac patient, nor did His soul or spirit appear like some sort of ghost, but His whole Person entered the reality of death, conquered it, and rose again in transfigured, divine power.

So what does that mean for us? It means we too are promised a resurrection. It means there is no need to fear death. Yet this is something it generally takes a lifetime to get our minds around. The martyrs, and those who suffer terminal illness at a young age, often seem to learn it quickly. It is precisely from their example of joy in the face of the last enemy that we too begin to learn what the Resurrection means.

We also learn from the faithful Fathers who gave us the liturgical celebrations. Have you noticed how the festal hymns often refer to historical events as present action? Even the Paschal greeting is "Christ *is* Risen! Indeed He *is* Risen!" and not "Christ rose from the dead once upon a time, or about two thousand years ago." Every Sunday at Matins we sing, "Having beheld the Resurrection of Christ, let us worship the Holy Lord Jesus . . ." as if we ourselves had been present in the garden that first Easter, and as if indeed that day were today!

Is this all just mental gymnastics, or a rather elaborate role-playing game, with sessions held every Sunday and feast-day? A non-believer might well think so, and even a Christian who does not have the Orthodox understanding of what the world is like might agree.

But to the Orthodox, life is sacramental. It is never only what it appears on the surface to be, but much more. The liturgical worship of the Church, and especially the Eucharist, is sacrament par excellence; but that sacramental view also runs through the most everyday and even seemingly trivial details of our lives.

At the Paschal Liturgy we sing, "As many as have been baptized into Christ have put on Christ! Alleluia!" Baptism, traditionally performed at Pascha, is the entry into a new life, a new life won for us by the Resurrection. The image of putting on Christ as a garment tells us He is both the protection and the glory of the baptized. To walk through life with Christ as a garment is to know that nothing is ordinary, nothing inconsequential, and nothing too fearful or burdensome to face.

I only made a few of these remarks, brief and tentative, to my fellow writer, and afterward thought deeper and in more detail. But in the sea of the true depth and richness of Pascha, these thoughts are mere grains of sand; the many wonderful writings of the Church Fathers, little more.

We read through the lectionary Sunday by Sunday, appropriating what little our human minds can begin to comprehend about the Resurrection, and celebrate the Paschal Feast with a joy that is but a faint echo of what we will know in the age to come. What does it mean? Everything, and the only thing, worth understanding; and like those disciples who accompanied Him on the road to Emmaus (Luke 24:13–35), we have a sense of being let in on a secret so great we scarcely dare to speak of it, our hearts burning with anticipation.

Bright Week

Red Shoes and White Robes

I HAVE NEVER BEEN MUCH FOR FASHION. I generally dress in what many writers and other at-home workers consider to be the uniform of their trade—blue jeans and a T-shirt, maybe a flannel shirt for cooler days. Still I appreciate the aesthetics of beautiful clothing, as long as I'm not the one who has to fuss about putting it together for myself.

They say that clothes make the man, or the woman. So I can cheer myself with the thought that wearing a writer's uniform ought to help make me a writer. Of course, it does depend what kind of writer we're talking about. I heard of one writer who taught herself to take her freelance days seriously by arriving at her home computer desk decked out in a business suit, hair coifed and makeup impeccably applied. At the opposite end of the spectrum, another writer, who did not care for the clock-punching approach, rhapsodized of her work, "You have not *lived* until you've known what it's like to go to work in your bathrobe!"

Clothing affects our view of ourselves. It also affects how others see us. I would not want to be in the, er, shoes, of any Hollywood actress stepping up in her Gucci gown to accept an award, if it would mean being on the receiving end of my daughters' sarcastic remark of "Nice dress she's almost wearing!"

In fact I do have a few preferences for clothing to wear to church—about the only place I go in something other than my writer's togs—and when the season's offerings happen to include things that suit me, I stock up, and then don't buy much more till my style comes around again some other year, by which time most of my wardrobe is looking a little drab. Then it's a pleasure to sport a new sweater or skirt in bright peacock blue, or a fresh lavender blouse or scarf.

Vanity is not one of my biggest temptations—my gluttony and sloth will trump it most any day. But there is one line I will not cross, one very personal craving I think it best to deny myself categorically. Perhaps it will seem odd to you, unless you have one such particular temptation of your own. My *verboten* bit of vanity is rooted deep in the reading of my childhood: whatever other apparel I indulge myself in, I can't bring myself to wear a pair of red shoes.

Do you remember the Hans Christian Andersen story? The little heroine, Karen, grows up very vain, and when it comes time to be confirmed after the Lutheran custom, she chooses red shoes to wear to church. "And while Karen knelt in the church she only thought of her red shoes; and she forgot to sing her psalm and forgot to say her prayer . . ." And when she comes out of the church, a magical punishment ensues, the shoes compelling her to dance and dance, until finally she is willing to undergo a deep repentance and learn true humility.

The problem, of course, was not the red shoes, but the little girl's attitude toward them. They were the symbol of her own vanity, and her desire to have people look at her and make her the center of attention—even at the most inappropriate times, such as when she ought to have been caring for her elderly benefactor instead of dancing at a ball, and above all at church when "the priest laid his hand upon her head and spoke the holy words. And the organ pealed solemnly, the children sang with their fresh sweet voices, and the old precentor sang too; but Karen thought only of her red shoes."

Our clothing ought to suit the occasion—and, for the Christian, it ought not to captivate our minds like this. Perhaps that is one reason for the simplicity of the white baptismal garments that were worn in ancient times by the newly-illumined in the week after Pascha, Bright Week. "As many as have been baptized into

Christ, have put on Christ," runs the joyful baptismal song, which we sing at Pascha and other baptismal feasts.

Think of putting on Christ like a garment! If we really gave our attention to this—not only at baptisms and in Bright Week, but all the time—what would it mean for us? How would we see ourselves, and how would others see us?

If we remembered that Christ is our cloak, would we get ourselves muddy with the everyday sins of pettiness and selfishness that so easily infest our lives?

Would we ever be afraid of anything, if we thought about Christ covering our nakedness, guarding us from the cold of the world and the bruising attacks of the enemy?

Would we try to show off and draw attention to ourselves, if we were obsessed with Christ as little Karen was obsessed with her red shoes, so that we could think of nothing else?

I don't know about anyone else, but I like to dress in my Sunday best for church, even here on the West Coast where casual clothing is the rule for almost everything. When I am invited to dine at the King's house, it would seem a little careless to turn up in my writer's uniform. For Pascha, especially, it seems only right to wear something new and festive as we celebrate the Resurrection, to show in our outward clothing as the clergy and baptismal candidates do with their gold and white, that our spirits are renewed.

But to put on Christ is to clothe not just our bodies but our souls in the Light that never fades. We do not put Him on at our baptism only to lay Him aside when Bright Week is over. To wear Christ as our Sunday best every day means to clothe our behavior with grace and kindness.

Are we self-centered? Let us clothe ourselves with the love and care Christ has for those around us. Are we vain? We must wear the cloak of Christ's humility as we go about our daily tasks, looking upon His image, instead of into a lying mirror.

The white robes of the newly-baptized in Bright Week symbolize the purity of new-washed souls in Christ. They represent light in the darkness, holiness in a world of sin. How wonderful this simplicity of spirit, far removed from the vacillations of fashion and the mirror-gazing of vanity. If we remind ourselves that we have indeed put on Christ, imagine the beauty of the dance our lives will make as we pass through this world—not, like the girl with the red shoes, compelled by an addictive self-love to endless and meaningless motion, but gracefully, purposefully, moving in joyful procession to carry Christ to others, as we shine in the flawless and glorious garment that is our Lord Himself.

Thomas Sunday

An Apostle's Hypothesis

EVERY SO OFTEN, AN ISSUE in the news will raise some sort of clash between science and religion, with ideas (and their proponents) grating and chafing against each other, throwing off sparks and raising hackles, and ultimately generating more heat than light.

The history of science and religion is a long and complex one, and many of the issues first raised in the Renaissance and Enlightenment are still unresolved today. We ought not to be surprised at this, for the tension between faith and knowledge undoubtedly goes back beyond recorded history. For Christians, it is perhaps most clearly exemplified in the Apostle Thomas, who is celebrated on this first Sunday after Resurrection in the Paschal cycle.

In the popular proverbial expression, this apostle is spoken of unflatteringly as the first "Doubting Thomas"; yet neither John's Gospel account nor the Orthodox liturgical text is so unkind to him—nor indeed to the phenomenon of unbelief itself.

Some years ago *The Georgia Straight*, Vancouver's entertainment weekly, published a cartoon portraying people entering a church and, as they did so, taking their brains out of their heads and depositing them in a box by the door marked "Check brains here." This scathing comment was the work of Dirk Van Stralen, himself a professing Christian grown weary with the entrenched attitudes of the evangelical subculture he had grown up in.

I think it's too bad the cartoonist chose a secular venue to make his point, as the world is already only too happy to hold the Faith as well as the faithful up to ridicule—but then again, perhaps he could get no hearing in the Christian community. A prophet has no honor in his own country.

The hymns of Thomas Sunday are a bit of an eye-opener in regard to this idea of "checking your brains at the door." In the hymns of the services, Thomas is looked on not with censure but with approval, because, like a good scientist, he is "curious" and "bold."

Thomas himself had made the hypothesis that if he might actually feel the Lord's wounded side, and the print of the nails in His hands, it would prove Jesus Himself was indeed risen from the dead, and not some mass hallucination of the demoralized Apostles, or a hoax they were trying to put over on the rest of the disciples. The Lord invited this apostle to touch His wounds and test his hypothesis. Thomas, not one of the others, was offered this privilege—and dared to accept it.

"O how praiseworthy and truly awesome is Thomas' undertaking! For daringly he touched the side that doth flash forth with the lightning of the divine fire" (Ode Five Troparion).

Jesus Himself does not condemn His doubtful disciple in the Gospel reading of the day (John 20:19–31); quite the opposite, in fact, as the hymns attest: "Thou didst rejoice when Thou wast examined. Wherefore, O Friend of man, Thou didst encourage Thomas in this, and didst show Thy side unto the disbelieving one, thereby assuring the world of Thine arising on the third day"(Matins Canon Ode Four Troparion).

It is perhaps the final words of the Gospel reading that many catch hold of, reading the rest of the story in their light, and drawing an unwarranted conclusion about Thomas and his unbelief: "Thomas, because you have seen Me, you believe. Blessed are those who have not seen and yet believe" (John 20:29).

Who has not seen and yet believes? Not the other Apostles. They too have seen—in fact, they saw before Thomas, because he was not there the first evening after the Resurrection, when the remaining ten disciples, closeted in fear of the authorities, suddenly had all their presuppositions blown away by Christ's entry into their midst through closed doors. Perhaps if places had been exchanged, the proverbial expression today might not be "Doubting Thomas," but "Doubting Peter" or "Doubting John" instead.

Who has not seen and yet believes? Many have done so down the ages, to this day; and for many, it is the testimony of the skeptical Thomas that helps them to belief, in the absence of seeing Christ resurrected with their own eyes. "Thou hast proved the disbelief of Thomas to be the mother of belief for us" (Ode Five).

Sometimes disbelief must precede true belief. It is little help to say to those suffering doubt, "Just believe!" Those who do believe without seeing are blessed indeed; but not everyone has that blessing. Saint Thomas is surely a comfort to those who find themselves not yet convinced.

Christ graciously condescended to Thomas's doubt; more, He singled him out for a very special experience . . . but not while he remained home alone with his doubt.

The Gospel and liturgical texts generously overlook the question, *Why was Thomas not with the others that first evening?* And that is because his absence, whatever his own motives, ultimately came about in God's providence. But it is clear he had to return to the fold in order to test his hypothesis. The tension between knowledge and faith could not be resolved from the outside. Only when he once more assembled with the rest of the Apostles was he there to meet Jesus and touch Him.

This is the beginning of the journey from unbelief to belief. To those who remain in doubt, the door of the church must be kept open. When the at-first skeptical Nathanael said, "Can anything good come out of Nazareth?" the Apostle Philip replied, "Come and see" (John 1:46). Unbelief sometimes has less to do with intellectual questions than it has to do with preconceptions or bad prior experiences of what the Church is all about. People in such situations must be invited to meet Jesus for themselves. To give them a tract or prayer to recite may or may not lead them to Him; better instead to invite them to follow the lead of Thomas, who began by insisting, "I will not believe, unless . . ." and, in the company of those gathered to wait on the Lord, ended by being the first to proclaim Christ "My Lord and my God!"

Sunday of the Myrrhbearers

Care of the Body

"I wish, O Son of the Living God . . . for a secret hut in the wilderness . . . a clear pool . . . a beautiful wood . . . a lovely church . . . a few sage disciples . . . and one room to go to for the care of the body, without wantonness, without voluptuousness, without meditation of evil."
—"The Wish of Manchán of Liath," tenth-century Irish

THIS LOVELY LITTLE ANCIENT IRISH POEM reveals the innocent, uncovetous desire of a hermit monk for a special dwelling place in the wilderness, where he may serve God. Envisioning his ideal hermitage, the speaker enumerates in simple delight the details that would content him—the forest for protection; a baptismal pool; a church with linen, Scriptures, candles; leeks, salmon, and bees for provisions; and an apostolic number of companions in worship. With delicacy but without shame, he does not fail to include in his wish a "room to go to for the care of the body."

Far from being "unspiritual," the care of the body is blessed by God. And those who provide for the bodily necessities of others, daily or extraordinarily, have a special ministry from God, one exemplified by the Myrrhbearing Women, as well as the Righteous Joseph of Arimathea, whom we commemorate on the second Sunday after Pascha. It is in fact very often women who perform the humble tasks associated with bodily need, sometimes with tremendous grace, as in the case of the woman who anointed Jesus' feet with perfume and washed them with her hair (John 12:1–8).

Feeding, clothing, cleansing, healing—we all of us must receive such ministrations at some time in our lives, beginning with our mother's milk. And we are all at the end in need of such final works of mercy as the Myrrhbearers wished to offer Jesus in anointing Him for His burial.

In the diversity of the Gospel accounts, it is not easy to identify definitively the number and names of these women, though it seems certain Mary Magdalene was one, while others mentioned by name include Salome and "Mary the mother of James" (Mark 15:40). In icons they sometimes appear as a crowd, sometimes as a symbolic three in number, paralleling the Magi who came to offer myrrh and other gifts at His Incarnation.

In the glitter of a church adorned with the iconographer's art, with the vested clergy processing and the choir singing, it is some-times easy to forget the blessedness of those who perform the less visible ministries in the service of Christ's Body—the retired man who cuts the church lawn; the woman who stocks the coffee cup-board in the church hall; even the Sunday school girl who wipes a smaller child's runny nose. Yes, even such a humble act is a conduit of grace, and anything but trivial if done in the name of Christ; and the one who performs it has an honorary place among the Myrrhbearers.

So often when we take on some task, our motives are quite mixed. We do things from fear of what others will think if we don't, or because we hope for some future benefit, or to be seen as self-sacrificing. But the Myrrhbearing Women went to the tomb with-out hope, and without any desire for recognition. They went only out of love because they could not bear to stay away—because this was the last thing left that they could do for their beloved Master, to anoint His body in death.

How might we carry out the simple daily ministration to the needs of God's people, if we thought this or that little thing, what-ever it might be, might be the last thing we could ever do for them?

The Myrrhbearers went to the tomb with love to perform one last task. How dreadful their disappointment at first to find this desire frustrated; indeed we see Mary Magdalene weeping and wondering, "Where have they laid my Lord?" (John 20:15). And then the awesome reversal of their plight and emotions, when the angel tells them, "He is risen! He is not here" (Mark 16:6).

Just think—if their love had not compelled them to perform their humble service to the Master's body, they would not have come to the Garden. But because, as the Lord teaches us to do (Luke 14:7–11), they had taken the humble place, they were now exalted and brought to the first rank. While Jesus' most trusted lieutenants, His chosen Apostles, hid in fear, these women went out into the dark before dawn to perform a task that must have seemed useless, more wasteful even than when Mary broke the vial of costly ointment on the Master's feet while He was still alive. A few women, intent upon the last thing that could be done for a dead man, became the first to know the good news that He was no longer dead.

This is the calling of us all in the Church, but some take to it more graciously than others. We minister to the Lord's Body, not only through the clerical service of liturgy, sacraments, and teaching, but also through ministering to the bodies of the members of Christ's Body. And we need to honor and appreciate those who do such little necessary services as are often noticed only when they are absent. Only let the "one room for the care of the body" attached to the church hall run out of bathroom tissue when you need to bring in your baby to change his diaper, and you will know how important these small details can be!

Let us then honor the Myrrhbearers who were first to know the Resurrection, and emulate them in our parishes. The humble tasks of service to Christ's Body are as precious as the gifts the Magi brought for His birth, a fragrant outpouring of love that leads us into the joyous triumph of His Resurrection.

Leavetaking of Pascha

Keeping God's Time

"THAT WENT FAST!"

Every year at Pascha, somebody in our parish makes this observation about the Lenten period just past. And every year as we take our leave of the Paschal season, again someone says, "That went fast!"

To be sure, there are times when it seems the forty-day fast will never end. Children moan, "Lentil soup again!," friends and spouses snap at each other, catechumens are suddenly assailed with doubts, and a pervasive weariness settles over us.

Then all of a sudden Holy Week gathers its momentum, like the Wolf inhaling prodigious lungsful of breath, holding a moment, then all in an instant blowing down the straw house. The services of the Bridegroom, the Twelve Gospels, the Winding-sheet, increase in length and intensity throughout the week, like labor pains; but when they are over, we can scarcely remember those dark and burdensome hours in the light of the newborn Pascha.

When the midnight feast is done, we go home utterly content to sleep, just as the birds are rising to praise God. But without effort we get up again in just a few hours to hunt eggs, turn on the TV for the first time in seven weeks (only to note that there's nothing worth watching!), and breakfast on leftover treats from our baskets. In the afternoon it's off to church again for Vespers and another community meal, and yet there never seems to be any hurry about this blessed day. God's time moves to its own beat, not to the rhythm of any artificial clock.

As Bright Week begins, the Paschal season stretches before us like the summer holidays before schoolchildren. In ancient times, and today in some traditions, all fasting is dispensed with in the forty days from Pascha to Ascension, though in many parishes today the practice is to resume Wednesday and Friday fasting after Bright Week. Still, in some Orthodox countries, Bright Week remains a true holiday, with time off work and school to attend services and to feast with friends and family. And yet however we celebrate the days between Pascha and Ascension, it seems the joyful Eastertide comes to an end too soon, and the choir laments, "This is the last time we get to sing 'The Angel Cried'!"

The Year of Grace of the Lord, by a Monk of the Eastern Church, tells us that "it is rare, if one has lived through the joy of Easter time sincerely, that one does not experience a certain constriction of the heart when the day of the Ascension comes." Yet, the Monk goes on to tell us, this should not be, for the disciples did not react this way, but rejoiced in Christ's glory in heaven. The Ascension, says the Monk, makes thoughts of heaven more immediate, more actual to us. Do we think of our permanent home often enough? he asks.

Author Madeleine L'Engle has produced a number of novels with interconnecting events and characters, but each falls into one of two streams which she calls by two different Greek terms for time: *kairos* and *chronos*. The *chronos* stories are realistic, contemporary stories that run on ordinary clock time, with nothing to raise the eyebrows of the skeptic. But the *kairos* tales encompass strange happenings, journeys through time and to other planets, and characters with surprising powers. They are tuned in to another world, another kind of time than the one that so easily meets and overwhelms our senses daily.

So I like to think of God in His outside-our-time heaven, His pure *kairos* where there are no alarm clocks or deadlines; and yet we know He also came into our ordinary, *chronos* time and place in the Incarnation. And I like to think those strange time effects of feasts and fasts are more than psychological; better, in fact, to call them sacramental. We feel the time has gone quickly, perhaps, because we have been so busy at our celebrations. But that dissonance between clock-and-calendar time and our apparently subjective feeling about the pace of time throughout the sacred seasons is more than just a subjective perception. It is a sign, a hint (and only one of many), that this world is not our home.

Ascension

Up and Down the Mountain

DESPITE THE GREETING-CARD WITTICISMS about being *over* the hill, I've invariably found that the road home leads *up*hill. In other words, things get tougher as we near our goals in life—that last push always seems to be the one that requires the most from us.

Maybe that's one reason why the Apostles had to climb up a mountain before the Ascension. I think this must be one of the most neglected feasts in our calendar; it has, after all, no special customs attached, such as the blessing of grapes at Transfiguration, nor is it one of the traditional baptismal feasts like Theophany, or Pascha itself. We tend to think of this holy day as something of a "comedown" in our Paschal celebrations, as the feasting ends and we enter a prayerful time of waiting for the descent of the Spirit at Pentecost. Yet Ascension is in fact the "climax of the climax," the *grand finale* of the Paschal event.

After the long dark vigil of that first Holy Friday and Saturday, the Resurrection burst upon the Apostles' despair in dazzling glory. From the depths of the pit, from the regions dark and deep, they were carried to a sudden and unexpected height. *The Kingdom!* they thought. *Our Master is going to bring in His Kingdom now—perhaps we will ride in His train to Jerusalem now, and this time not on a humble donkey . . .*

But no. Instead of leading them into Jerusalem, He *sends* them, on a new pilgrimage—after they had thought they were done, all the darkness and toil swallowed up in the victory of the Resurrection—after all this, they must go back to Galilee where they began.

And then they have to climb a mountain! And no, He does not lead them—He promises instead to *meet* them there, after they have walked there and, by faith, scaled the mountain.

We must remember the word *climax* has the same root as *climb*. Ascension truly is the climax of the Paschal season, the final seal on the faith of the Apostles who obeyed the Lord's command to make this mountain pilgrimage. His going into heaven in their very sight was final proof of His divinity, His return to where He came from. The Resurrection was joy and power and the turning of darkness to light; but while Jesus remained with them on earth, whatever miracles He wrought, He would still appear to be an earthly Messiah seeking an earthly kingdom. The Ascension places the final nail in the coffin of that misapprehension.

They stood gazing up into heaven in amazement. One imagines they were a little stunned—*You're going, Lord? But—but—*

But they've learned from experience that when He makes a promise, it is fulfilled. *Meet me at the mountain—I'll be there.* And He was. *Go on back to Jerusalem now, and stay there—I'll send you My Spirit.*

Mountaintops have a long history in God's dealings with His people, most notably in the case of Moses communing with God, receiving the Ten Commandments on Mount Sinai and bringing them back down to the Israelites. And let's not forget Noah—the ark landed upon a mountaintop and, like Moses, Noah afterward came down from the mountaintop, transformed, to a new life and way of living.

Our Lord, however, as so often is shown in the Gospel accounts, walks the same road as the prophets of old, only to turn the expectations of observers on their heads. As our Lord blesses His disciples, instead of coming *down* the mountain, He *ascends* out of their sight into heaven on a cloud—and *they* are the ones who must come down the mountain they climbed in such toil and hope!

At last they understand He is no earthly King. Nor is He merely a God-sent prophet; this, they realize, is the role *they* are called upon to fill. They, with the all-too-human weaknesses revealed to them in Holy Week (*You will deny me, Peter*) are to come down the mountain like Moses and preach to the people.

Up and down the mountain. This was the obedience given the Apostles, and so it is ours too. When we make the arduous upward pilgrimages of life, learning and growing by experience, it is not for us to stand too long gazing into heaven thinking, Alleluia! We made it! The Lord got us through this terrible vale of misery—through this pain or illness, this loss of a loved one, this disappointment or test. We must come back down that mountain, because we are His prophets, His sent ones, like heroes returning from a quest to share what we have gained. And the prize we have won on this quest is none other than the Pearl of Great Price, the Lord Himself.

I would just as soon stay on the mountaintop, myself—the air is clear, and there aren't too many crowds. When you go back down, as often as not you find people who don't want to hear about the mountaintop—like the ancient Israelites, they are too busy worshiping idols. And then, too, there is the sheer dejection in coming back down. We have run the race, finished the course, the taste of victory is sweet as we plant our flag on the summit. Who could wish to go back down again?

There is one thing to make the descent bearable, the one thing by which we can do anything—our Lord's promise given in Acts 1:8, which we know will be kept: "You shall receive power when the Holy Spirit has come upon you; and you shall be My witnesses."

Part VIII

Pentecost, Season of the Spirit

Pentecost

Fire at Pentecost

FIRE FOR US IS EASY. A flick of a lighter, or even the push of a button, and a picture-perfect fire is burning placidly in our modern hearths. If you have no hearth, never mind—you can get a virtual fire in the form of a videotape, complete with the sound of the crackling and popping of wood.

For the ancients, though, it was a matter of patient labor to bring forth sparks from flint, feeding the kindling with their breath. Or they might preserve a fire they already had, carefully banking the ashes at night to be stirred and resurrected into flames in the morning. Apart from these, there was only one way to get fire: to wait for lightning to strike.

The untamable power of the lightning bolt could suddenly consume whatever it struck; yet without fire, man would be condemned to live as an animal—no cooking, no blacksmithery, no defense against the predators of night or the cold of winter. Fire seems something not quite of this world; it can fall from the sky in a blaze of destruction, or elevate and transform everyday life by its mysterious consuming, heat- and light-giving power. It is no accident that God in the Old Testament is associated with storm and fire (e.g. Psalm 18:7–15).

In our post-industrial world, we think we understand fire because we know it is a chemical process, a matter of atoms and molecules. A few people—firefighters among them—know it is more. The film *Backdraft* gives a few hints about fire's transcendent character, but those of us sitting in the audience are not easy to impress.

Almost daily we see pyrotechnic explosions on the news or in the movies, and they do not go to our hearts, for they are carefully confined to the screen, with the volume turned down. How then can we begin to imagine what it felt like to be there on the Day of Pentecost?

They had been waiting ten days, since Jesus ascended into heaven, for the Spirit He had promised. Waiting for God's lightning to strike.

"And suddenly there came a sound from heaven, as of a rushing mighty wind, and it filled the whole house where they were sitting. Then there appeared to them divided tongues, as of fire, and *one* sat upon each of them," Saint Luke writes in the Acts of the Apostles (2:2, 3).

God's own special effects, these. But they did not simply dazzle the eyes. With the flames came a supernatural gift of language, a reversal of the ancient curse of Babel, corroborated by witnesses who had come to Jerusalem for the Jewish feast from throughout the known world. They heard these untaught Galileans, country hicks, speaking in numerous tongues about the wonderful works of God.

The tongues of fire settled upon the disciples, but like the burning bush encountered by Moses, these human vessels were not consumed. Yet we must not think they were untouched. They were in fact so profoundly transformed that they were no longer confined only to the language they had known from the cradle. They could begin to speak in languages they had never learned. They spoke nothing but the praise of God, for, like the Prophet Isaiah with the coal touched to his lips, they had been purified by flame (Isaiah 6:6, 7).

Not just at Pentecost, but every day, Orthodox Christians pray for the Holy Spirit to come upon them, in the prayer, "O Heavenly King," asking that He "cleanse us from every impurity." How dare we? Do we really want a "rushing mighty wind" to sweep in and set flames upon our heads? If we do, we must be prepared to do as the embryonic Church did: continue "with one accord in prayer and supplication." The flames of the Spirit descended on each individual, but only when they had first assembled together.

We need the patience of waiting for lightning to strike, the persistence of breathing our prayers out upon the kindling of our souls until they catch. And then what will happen?

The Apostle Peter warns us, "Do not think it strange concerning the fiery trial which is to try you. . . . If you are reproached for the name of Christ, blessed *are you*, for the Spirit of glory and of God rests upon you" (1 Peter 4:12, 14).

Read the Book of Acts to see how the fire of God's Spirit burns. See how the Spirit draws the openhearted, Jew and Gentile, with the warmth of love diffused through the disciples. See how He strikes in flaming judgment when Ananias and Sapphira lie to the Apostles. See how He puts the beasts of night, the demons, to flight with His incandescent power. And see, yes, how He refines the pure gold of the Church in the furnace of martyrdom.

Thrilling, but a little frightening, isn't it? Let me leave you with a last thought in the form of a haiku I wrote some years ago:

you must be prepared
if you pray for holy fire to
get your hair singed.

Sunday of All Saints

The Hidden Season of the Church Year

THE MORE I STUDY THE CALENDAR and seasons of the Church, the more I am aware of an interesting paradox: though there is a profound order to our Orthodox life, it is never perfectly tidy! This is undoubtedly the action of the Holy Spirit in the history of the Church, for "the Wind blows where it will."

For example, the way the Paschal season flows into that of Pentecost is perhaps a little surprising. From the day of Pascha itself, in place of the usual epistle readings, we hear already the Acts of the Apostles—which, I believe, might equally well be titled, "The Acts of the Holy Spirit," as the Apostles attest with the phrase, "it seemed good to the Holy Spirit, and to us . . ." (Acts 15:28). So when the fiftieth day after Pascha finally comes, and we are to celebrate the coming of the Holy Spirit, we have already read about the action of the Spirit in the Church.

Next, although we celebrate a "leavetaking" of Pentecost after just one festal week, "I am with you always," says our Lord, this being why He gave the Spirit, the Comforter. Therefore, instead of Pentecost being neatly closed off as we move on to other dogmatic topics, the Church provides a way for this season of the Spirit to remain with us much longer, by continuing to number each week from Pentecost until we again take up the Triodion at the beginning of next Lent. In fact the remembrance of Pentecost and the Holy Spirit remains with us daily in the prayer, "O Heavenly King, the Comforter, the Spirit of Truth . . ."

Christ is with each of His people in the Spirit, but always through the Church, the saints, and our fellow Christians, never in isolation—not even in the case of solitary mystics who are granted to see Uncreated Light, for they would testify to the aid they receive from the prayers of the saints and of their brethren. It is therefore no accident that the Sunday of All Saints comes one week after Pentecost.

The Western All Saints Day is celebrated along with the remembrance of All Souls at the end of October—hence "Hallowe'en," the Eve of All Hallows (meaning saints or holy ones), which historically clashed with the pagan culture around it. It was a Christian celebration of the glorified occurring at the same time as a pagan one honoring the dead, at the season when the year itself dies in the Northern hemisphere. While it is always useful to celebrate holiness, and especially so in the face of darkness (Christmas was instituted for similar reasons), the Eastern calendar shows more clearly how the sanctity of the saints flows from the gift of the Holy Spirit.

Additionally, the Sunday following this one is set aside to honor particular regional or national saints. And this leads us into what I call the "hidden season of the Church year," the season of the saints that lasts all year long.

There is not a day of the year that does not celebrate numerous saints. Some you will not hear of in your North American parish, while they may be the chief patrons of some small village in Eastern Europe or the Mediterranean. Others will be famous and beloved of the whole Church everywhere, like Saint Nicholas, who is commemorated not only on December 6 but also with the Apostles on Thursday of every week. Only the names and dates of martyrdom are recorded of many Christians from the early centuries; of the lives of more recently canonized saints, such as Innocent of Alaska, there is often extensive documentation.

Apostles, prophets, patriarchs, hierarchs, ascetics, wonderworkers, martyrs, confessors—some saints fit more than one of the many categories, while some designations, such as teachers and fools for Christ, appear to be mutually exclusive. Certain female saints, such as Mary Magdalene, are given the title "Equal to the Apostles" to acknowledge the greatness of their contribution to Christ's Church; while many other women of God, like Saint Monica, mother of Augustine, are best known in their character of divine humility, for their roles in nurturing others into sainthood. The more we learn of the many varieties of God's holy ones, the more we understand this untidiness of the Spirit blowing wherever He wills. Even the short accounts we have in Scripture of patriarchs like David and apostles like Peter show us the individual characters, quite complete with faults, of those who are chosen to be vessels for the Spirit. And what good news that is for us.

It is noteworthy that the word "season" comes from the Latin root meaning "seed" or "to sow." As a famous phrase aptly puts it, "the blood of the martyrs is the seed of the Church." While the great seasons of the Church and of nature turn about the year, seed-time, harvest, death, and resurrection, each day brings us a little season, the lives and deaths of saints then commemorated.

By reading their lives with our children, or perhaps communally in our parishes after services such as Vespers, and by remembering to ask the prayers of those saints of the day in our individual prayers, we can celebrate this blessed "season." In so doing, we shall plant the Pentecostal seed, the action of the Spirit, in our own lives as they have in theirs.

The Apostles' Fast and Feast

Feast of the Mismatch

WHEN THE EXUBERANCE OF PASCHA and Pentecost have run their course, when Ascension has capped the celebrations with its sublime vision of our Lord's return to His heavenly throne, it is time at last to get down to the business of living out our faith again in an everyday way. So then what is this that greets us only ten days after the Leavetaking of Ascension? Yet *another* fast!

Each of the four yearly fasting seasons has its own purposes and character, but the fast of Peter and Paul is set apart from the others in some ways. Not as stringent or as strongly penitential as Great Lent or the Dormition Fast, it leads up to a feast (June 29) not belonging to the cycle of Twelve Great Feasts which honor our Lord or His Mother and recount salvation history.

The Feast of Peter and Paul itself is ancient. Some early sources assume the date honors their martyrdom together in the persecution of Nero, while others claim it refers to the translation of their relics some two centuries later. The Church of Rome, in exalting the papal claims, afterward shifted St. Paul's feast to the following day so as to have the original commemoration dedicated to Peter alone, but the Orthodox Church has always maintained the fitness of honoring the two great apostles together.

My husband (I'll admit it—I stole some material for this column from one of his sermons!) calls this the Feast of the Mismatch. He points out that these two saints had such different backgrounds and personalities, they might have been voted "least likely to appear together on an icon." But that is just where they do appear—and, most notably, they hold between them a model church.

This is the sort of icon often used to portray the patron or patrons of a local temple, but in the case of the icon of Peter and Paul, the significance of the symbolism is much wider. Alike in apostolic calling but vastly different in background, personality, and fields of service, Peter and Paul stand for us as the patrons and servants of the Holy Church's unity.

Peter, a poor, unrefined fisherman, blustery and hotheaded, one of the first-called and inner circle of Jesus' disciples, went to the Jews. Paul, a brilliant and highly educated Roman citizen of focused energy, had to be knocked off his horse by a divine vision to turn him from persecuting the Church and transform him into the chief apostle to the Gentiles. Paul tells us in his letter to the Galatians (2:11ff.) how he was forced to give Peter a public dressing-down on the issue of his behavior toward the newly converted Gentiles. But even after such a sharp disagreement, they parted finally at peace and in unity to serve Christ in their diverse ministries.

So today "ethnic" and "convert," monastic and parish/city church may sometimes have to go their separate ways, but there ought to be no need or excuse for jealousy or the pride of schism. Within the local community, too, there is room for the same kind of vigorous debate and, if necessary, correction, as occurred between Peter and Paul in the context of the apostolic college.

What there is not room for is pettiness. This is why a fast before this feast is so fitting, and a pointer to the unique kind of asceticism only possible in community.

We often think of asceticism chiefly in terms of hermit saints like Mary of Egypt, fasting and praying in desert solitude; but in a community setting we sometimes see more openly the spiritual *askesis* that is symbolized and assisted by the bodily *askesis* of fasting. The local community, whether monastic or parish, is something like a rock tumbler, a barrel-like machine in which small stones are rotated in water for long periods of time until they are polished to a decorative shine. Like the tumbler, the asceticism of community is meant not to wear us down, but to wear the rough edges off all of us as we get knocked against each other by our daily and weekly life together as the fellowship of the baptized.

Askesis is discipline—chiefly found in such forms of self-denial as fasting, prostrations, and vigils. These things can be done either alone or in community. But *only* in community can we also deny ourselves in such other ways as learning consideration for others; forgiving when they are not considerate of us; serving the community with labor, such as the upkeep of our church and hall; bringing and sharing of our substance for the financial needs of the parish or for the community meal; or giving of our time to help with child care, Sunday school, transportation, or office work. These are only a few of the possible avenues for self-denial in our local church bodies, for as God multiplies our parishes by baby booms, conversions, immigration, or transfers to the area, so He also multiplies opportunities to rub shoulders—and rub off sharp edges—with our fellow believers.

Only in community do we recognize how manifold and wonderful is God's creation of those icons He himself has made, the sons and daughters of Adam and Eve. Jew or Gentile, educated or uneducated, male, female, great-grannies, teenage boys, babes in arms, and middle-aged couples; CEO or welfare case, scholar or mechanic, wheelchair-bound or Olympic athlete, God makes us all to serve His various purposes. He makes both the Marys and the Marthas—He makes us all with different gifts of personality, experience, and inclination.

It is only our fallen state that makes these differences a cause of friction. But in community, even friction can be used by God to polish us like stones in the tumbler.

Yet *another* fast? Yes, a very special fast and feast. If we keep the unity of Peter and Paul in mind, the *askesis* of community will in time wear us smooth, and we will shine, beautiful gems fit to be placed together in the walls of the Heavenly City.

Part IX

A Christian Ending

August 1
Cross Procession

A Trustworthy Sign

"TRUST YOUR FEELINGS, LUKE."

A classic line delivered by Sir Alec Guinness, in the role of the wise old mentor Obi-Wan Kenobi. It is a succinct summary of a life-philosophy for an entire generation. The 1970s, which gave birth to the *Star Wars* saga, were known as the "Me Generation." Predictably, the focus on "me, me, me" led to the all-out consumerism of the 1980s.

When the economy sputtered and stalled, people began to look to the opposite of materialism for satisfaction, so in the 1990s the New Age movement shuffled into town. Decade after decade, the world trusts its feelings, wandering sheeplike toward greener pastures, without ever asking the question, "How can I know that my feelings are trust*worthy*?"

I saw *Star Wars* when it first came out in theaters in the 1970s, and have been fond of it ever since. But its themes of courage, heroism, and loyalty seem to have been neglected by a society of lost individuals intent upon pursuing the will-o'-the-wisp of their own feelings.

"My feelings!" A girl in a British Columbia high school last year felt like baring her skin to the waist. So she did. A boy who saw her felt like making a lewd remark in response—so he did. The girl then felt disrespected, and complained to the school administration. I don't know how the boy felt after he got disciplined, and she didn't.

They both trusted their feelings. But apparently, despite our society's urging them to do just that, one of them at least was wrong to do so.

I can't imagine Princess Leia stripping off her bra in public just because she felt like it, or Luke doing anything but blushing if she or any other young woman did so in his presence. But in our society, confusion reigns in such matters, because "feelings" have been elevated to the level of Holy Writ.

Of course when Obi-Wan told Luke to trust his feelings, he was talking about the ability the Force gave him to hit a seemingly impossible target. But unlike the Jedi knight's fantasy powers, our everyday feelings are not based on scientifically measurable "midichlorians" in the bloodstream.

Feelings in the real world are a peculiar mix of numerous factors, including hormones, upbringing, prejudices, prior experience, fears, peer pressure, wishful thinking, the state of our health, the phase of the moon, the time of year, what we ate for our last meal, and how much sleep we got last night.

This is quite graphically demonstrated to us every time we take part in one of the Church's fasting periods. It usually doesn't take more than a very little hunger, tiredness, or boredom to turn our moods upside-down.

We clearly can *not* trust our feelings. How then are we to find our way in life? What unchanging standard, what sure sign will mark the path of our pilgrimage?

The Church gives us the answer in the Feast of the Procession of the Cross, which inaugurates the Dormition Fast. This commemoration of the Holy Cross is one of three in the Church Year (the others are September 14, the Exaltation of the Cross, and the Sunday of the Cross at Mid-Lent). The particular focus of this one on August 1, says the Monk of the Eastern Church in his book, *The Year of Grace of the Lord*, "concerns 'following the Cross where it leads us, and thus forms the practical outcome of the previous feasts.' "

To follow the Cross. If Christians really believed it to be their only sure sign in life, ninety percent of the "Christian" books being published these days would disappear from the store shelves. You cannot follow the Cross and have your eyes on the same goals as the yuppies of the 1980s. You cannot follow the Cross while seeking after signs and wonders, persuading yourself that because you claim to love Jesus, you will avoid the deceptions of the New Agers. And you cannot follow the Cross if you keep your attention steadfastly upon "me, me, me" and "my feelings."

Because the Cross marches at the head of a funeral procession. Those who followed it on missionary journeys to distant lands left behind the comforts of family and civilization, many of them never to return. Those who followed it to the arenas of Rome and the Soviet *gulags* divested themselves of every self-interest.

Death and taxes, goes the cliché, are inevitable. The world recoils from and avoids the Cross, for it points to the inevitability of the grave. But we have the blessing of this Festal Procession as we make our way towards the Dormition of our Lord's Mother, her good death which models the true Christian death for us.

We cannot trust our feelings. But we can trust the Cross, for it is Christ's gift to us—in the words of the Kontakion of the Cross, "the invincible weapon of His peace," the sign that will never lead His sheep astray.

August 6
Transfiguration

Dead People and Dumb People

"I SEE DEAD PEOPLE. They don't even know that they're dead."
This fearful whisper comes from the young boy at the center of the
supernatural thriller, *The Sixth Sense*. What an image of our own
world this is. If we could see the things that really surround us, we
too would be scared—not of fictitious ghosts made horrifying by
cinematic special effects, but of dread heavenly powers, engaged in
battle with the minions of the rebellious evil one. It is thanks to
God's mercy that, in the normal course of events, we cannot see the
world and its inhabitants as they really are, or we would be constantly paralyzed with fear.

But occasionally God chooses to open our spiritual eyes. The
Transfiguration of Our Lord on the mountain was one of those
occasions. Only His inner circle of disciples witnessed this momentous revelation of Jesus' true nature, and even they were hardly able
to make sense of it—because, like all of us, they looked at the world
generally with spiritually blinded eyes.

The disciples, like the rest of the world, saw Jesus as many things.
They knew or believed that He was the promised Messiah. They
understood that He was a great Teacher. They even saw Him do
miracles, which they believed was by the power of God, though
His enemies tried to explain them away. But how far short of
reality were any of these things which they thought they saw and
understood!

And so that day came the luminous vision—or rather, the apostles' eyes were unveiled to see the reality of the spiritual world beyond the material one, the glorious light shining from the Heavenly King who walked the earth as a humble teacher, and at His side two great members of His celestial court, Moses and Elijah, shining along with Him.

The most tremendous thing about this story, to me, is not the picture of heavenly light blazing at the top of an ordinary, earthly hill, but rather the astonishingly inappropriate response of Peter, who says, "Lord, let's make three tabernacles here, one for you, one for Moses and one for Elijah" (Mark 9:5). Despite the heavenly revelation, Peter was still seeing things in an earthly way, thinking of Jesus as just one more of the leaders of Israel, along with the likes of Elijah and Moses.

We must be grateful that St. Matthew records how the apostle gloriously missed the mark on this one, because if it can happen to the saints, we shouldn't be surprised that it happens to us too. I can't help thinking here of a parody of the line from *The Sixth Sense* that's been making the rounds on the net. A still of the little boy speaking to Bruce Willis comes attached with the caption: "I see dumb people. They don't even know that they're dumb!"

Why are they, and we, "dumb"? Because we persist in seeing spiritual things in fleshly ways. Because even on those rare occasions when we are granted to catch some glimpse of spiritual insight, we are so eager to run with it to some entirely wrong-headed conclusion. And most of all because we don't even know we're being dumb.

We are enslaved to our outward perceptions. We think less of ourselves if our faces, our bodies, our mannerisms fail to match those that are touted as ideal on TV and in fashion magazines. We extend that prejudice towards others, sometimes cruelly, as you can learn from any schoolchild who is seen by his peers as too short, too fat, the wrong color, or not dressed right. We vote for politicians who are tall or have strong chins, regardless of party or policy. We impute wrong motives to our neighbors, when we scarcely understand why we ourselves do the things we do. We are dumb, and don't even know it.

Years ago my husband gave an arresting object lesson during a sermon. He held up a freshly cut carnation, fragrant and bursting with color. "Beautiful, isn't it?" he remarked. *"But it's dead."*

If you are thinking of seeing *The Sixth Sense* and don't want it spoiled, stop reading now, because I am going to reveal the surprise ending here.

The carnation was dead—why? Because it had been cut off from its source. It appeared as beautiful as before it had been cut, but soon it was going to wilt and wither.

In *The Sixth Sense*, Bruce Willis is investigating and trying to help the little boy who sees dead people, people who don't even know they're dead. Willis is so obsessed with the mystery and his work that his estrangement from his wife and from all other aspects of his life increases throughout the film—until he realizes the truth: *he himself is one of the dead people.* He didn't notice the difference at first because his life before was already so devoid of real involvement. He was already like a dead man when he was still alive.

That is the tragedy of human beings in our world today who go busily about their lives, unaware as cut carnations that they are dead, cut off from their Source of Life, the Lord. They do not have the eyes to see the hidden reality of who Jesus really is.

We who serve Christ are not dead any longer. We are risen in Christ, baptized into Christ, we have received the Heavenly Spirit. All too often, though, we are still a little bit dumb. But perhaps when we think of Peter and the others at the Transfiguration, we can at least remember and *know* that we are dumb. God mercifully passed over Peter's dumb response at the Transfiguration without rebuke, and instead pointed him and the other apostles toward the essential thing: "This is My beloved Son, in whom I am well pleased. Hear Him!"

August 15
Dormition of the Theotokos

Triumph over Tragedy

THE CELEBRATION OF THE DORMITION of the Theotokos lay two weeks behind us when we set out for church one Sunday morning some years ago. As we pulled out of the driveway, the radio announced in shocked tones the death of Princess Diana in a high-speed car accident in France.

Of course the Princess of Wales was remembered at Liturgy, but I did not stay afterward to discuss the news. My girls had been taking part in a Shakespearean workshop for young people, and we had to hurry off to their performance, in which they would share the role of Ophelia with two other girls in the tragedy of *Hamlet*. The play was the thing, and the girls had to prepare to "hold a mirror up to nature."

Undoubtedly the most famous of Shakespeare's plays—and the most difficult—*Hamlet* holds the mirror up to that central mystery of human existence, death. In the week following Diana's death, as the crash was decried and speculated upon around the world, the word "tragedy" was much in evidence. The media have no better word to use for some sad event, and certainly in this sense Diana's death was a tragedy; but in the Shakespearean sense, tragedy is not defined by death itself or death alone. It is not merely a character's death that is tragedy so much as his or her life—the events and choices, and most of all the tragic character flaws, that lead to his or her downfall. Death is only the culmination of the character's acts.

While this view of tragedy may or may not describe Diana (depending on which speculations you choose to believe about her life story), tragedy in the Shakespearean sense is certainly an apt description of the story of Adam. Pride and disobedience lead to banishment from the garden, and to death being let loose in the world.

From the perspective of Orthodox Christianity, though, this fundamental tragedy of human nature, our slavery to sin and death, is only the beginning of the story. You only have to experience Holy Week and Pascha once to sense the enormous triumph of Life over Death in the Resurrection of Christ.

Faith in the next life is easy at Pascha, but we Orthodox, like everyone else, must hold funerals for our lost loved ones; not only for those who perhaps have wasted away for many years while we cared for them and whose passing is an apparent mercy, but also sometimes for those young and full of promise, or for those we never imagined ourselves living without.

The Dormition or Falling Asleep of the Theotokos is the ideal of a Christian death. How astonishing it is to hear the canticles of the feast, not mourning, but vigorously celebrating her departure for the next life:

"Thy sacred and renowned memorial, O Virgin, is clothed in the embroidered raiment of divine glory. It has brought the faithful together in joy, and led by Miriam, with dances and timbrels, they sing the praises of thine Only-begotten Son . . ."

A joy incomprehensible to the world permeates this service, light-years removed from *Hamlet* and from Princess Diana's state funeral. Days after her shocking death, crowds outside Westminster Abbey poured out an intense grief unfamiliar to the reserved British character, and bemoaned their part in consuming the wares of the *paparazzi*. And yet, unless we die as the Theotokos did, in the bosom of Christ, our own deaths, even if they come quietly to us in advanced age, will be no less tragic than Diana's, or than the fictional deaths in *Hamlet*.

It gave me great pause to hear a Byzantine-style chant of "Alleluia" accompanying Diana's lily-laden casket as it processed down the aisle, like Ophelia floating down the river. It was Orthodox composer John Tavener's "Song for Athene," originally written for the funeral of a friend of his who had died accidentally; and once again I was astonished to find a connection to *Hamlet,* in its opening line: ". . . May flights of angels sing thee to thy rest."

A brief note of hope at the conclusion of a bleak and disturbing play. The best, perhaps, that many of us can manage sometimes in the face of death, our own death or that of our loved ones. One hears of saintly people who pass to the next life in joy and peace, imparting the glow of faith to all around them, so that the bereaved know a true joy mingled with the sorrow of losing a loved one. Too often, however, it is not so, and death finds us as unprepared as the princess in the car crash and her many mourners.

This perhaps is the purpose of the Feast of Dormition. We do not simply *remember* that the Theotokos entered into the resurrection as the ideal of a Christian death; we are called to celebrate, each year. My daughters rehearsed full days for weeks before the performance of their play; for the Orthodox Christian, the Feast of Dormition is our rehearsal for our passage from earth to heaven, for "the tomb becomes a ladder," as the services say.

Shakespeare and Tavener both got one important detail right. We are not alone at our death. The angels will accompany us, just as we see they do the Theotokos in the icon of her Dormition.

Meanwhile, let us be mindful of the need to prepare for death as we pray at every Liturgy for "a Christian ending to our life, painless, blameless, and peaceful; and a good defense before the dread judgment seat of Christ." And let us give all our strength to the rehearsal of our future performance in the heavenly spectacle, our partaking of Christ's triumph over tragedy, by celebrating the Dormition of His Mother with all the extravagance urged upon us by the songs for the feast:

"Let every mortal born on earth, carrying his torch, in spirit leap for joy, and let the order of the angelic powers celebrate and honor the holy feast."

Conclusion

Till We Get It Right

THE STORY IS TOLD OF A NEW PRIEST who is assigned to a parish that has a history of bickering and discord. His first homily is on the topic, "Love one another" (John 13:34). It sounds good to them. As they get his blessing on the way out of church they say, "Lovely homily, Father."

But next Tuesday the same people are at each other's throats at the parish council meeting. Father says nothing.

The following Sunday, he gives the same sermon, word for word. Some of the people were asleep last week, so they don't really notice. A few of them blink and wonder if this new priest is quite all right in the head. But they get his blessing and thank him for the homily anyway, as before.

During the week, Father is invited to the Sisterhood meeting. They conduct their business, ask Father to pronounce the blessing, and break up for tea. Father is such a quiet sort that some of them forget he's there and start gossiping about their neighbors. Father says nothing but, you guessed it, he trots out that same sermon at Sunday Liturgy, "Love one another."

This goes on for several more weeks until at last the parish council calls an emergency meeting, with just one item on the agenda. They confront their pastor: "When are we going to get a new sermon, Father?"

Father smiles. "Just as soon as you've learned to put this one into practice!"

This same lesson seems to be echoed in the cycle of the Church year. We come to the Church's New Year every September, and I for one have sometimes wondered—how can anything be "new" when we do it over and over again?

It reminds me of the Bill Murray film *Groundhog Day*. Murray plays the part of a cynical, egocentric weather reporter assigned to cover the emergence of Punxatawny Phil, the weather-forecasting groundhog, from his winter den. The Murray character goes through the day in his usual temper, trampling other people's feelings underfoot like the snow that covers the streets of the town. At day's end he goes to bed, eager to get back to the big city the next day; but when his alarm rings, strange things begin to happen.

The radio is playing the same song as the day before. And the announcers are talking about Groundhog Day, *today, February second!* The hapless Murray proceeds through the day in nearly the same manner as the day before, meeting the same people, having virtually the same interactions. He knows beforehand whether the groundhog will see its shadow, knows which kinds of food people will choose to eat . . . he is living the *same day* once again.

When the alarm rings next morning and the same song plays on the radio yet again, he knows he is trapped. He begins to experiment, to see what he can change. He begins to be attracted to a co-worker and as a result starts to behave at least a little more politely toward her. Yet once again, he awakens the next morning to another rerun of Groundhog Day. There follows a long and arduous spiritual journey, as all Murray's efforts lead to no substantive change in the events of the day. He is tempted to despair, and commits "suicide" several days in a row—and still wakes up to yet another Groundhog Day the next morning.

Then he embarks on a mission of self-improvement, and this is where the film reminds me most of the strong ascetic character of Orthodoxy. He becomes disciplined and open-minded, learning to play piano and studying poetry.

But most importantly, he turns his attention away from himself and begins to actively look for opportunities to help other people. In the end, it is the giving and receiving of love that break him free of the endless cycle of Groundhog Day after Groundhog Day.

Some commentators have likened this film to an eastern religious idea of reincarnation, while others have pointed out that the character's experience resembles purgatory. But our Orthodox calendar gives us this experience of repeating certain events annually, right here in this life, over and over "till we get it right."

The Church New Year can make us especially aware of this. St. Symeon Stylites, celebrated on the New Year's Day of September 1, must have lived nearly every day on his pillar in a seemingly repetitious manner, watching the sun come up, and watching the sun go down. Yet he made the inward journey to spiritual maturity without moving from that pillar for thirty-six years.

The Church New Year is a good time for parishes to hold prayer services, and for individuals to go to confession. It is a better time, I feel, than the secular New Year for making "resolutions," reviewing our life of the previous year, setting goals for the year ahead, and generally "taking stock." For the past few years I have had a brief list of goals I hoped to accomplish in the year ahead, and though I have fallen short of perfection each time, I did make progress I am convinced I would never have made without focusing my intent at the beginning of the Church Year.

Whether or in what manner each of us does something like this is an individual decision. However, the one imperative for us is the same one expressed by the new priest in the tale we heard, and in *Groundhog Day*: "Love one another." It is the message of one of the most famous passages of scripture, the thirteenth chapter of Paul's First Epistle to the Corinthians. Like the man in the movie, I can learn to play the piano, I can do all kinds of good deeds, but whatever my accomplishments, "if I have not love, I am nothing."

It is a lesson it takes us humans a lifetime to learn, and in God's mercy the Church guides us through the steps year by year, as we learn the history of God's love for us in His Incarnation, Death, and Resurrection, and of the love of His saints, our examples, in response to His divine love. Let us keep this lesson in mind, as we begin this Church New Year, and every New Year thereafter, until at last we "get it right."

For Further Reading
About the Seasons of the Orthodox Church

Fr. Alexander Schmemann, *Great Lent*, St. Vladimir's Seminary Press

A Monk of the Eastern Church, *The Year of Grace of Our Lord,* St. Vladimir's Seminary Press

Frederica Mathewes-Green, *Facing East*, HarperSanFrancisco

Bishop Kallistos Ware and Mother Mary, trans., *The Lenten Triodion*, Faber & Faber Ltd.

Bishop Kallistos Ware and Mother Mary, trans., *The Festal Menaion*, Faber & Faber Ltd.

Holy Transfiguration Monastery, *The Pentecostarion*

Fr. Thomas Hopko, *The Winter Pascha*, St. Vladimir's Seminary Press

Liturgical Booklet Series, Department of Religious Education, Orthodox Church in America

Other Books of Interest from Conciliar Press

Journey to the Kingdom: Reflections on the Sunday Gospels
by Fr. John Mack

An excellent companion to *Seasons of Grace*, these reflections on the Sunday Gospels by Fr. John Mack are imbued with both patristic and biblical wisdom.

In *Journey to the Kingdom*, we are taken lovingly through the Church Year with the stories of the lives of saints, as well as observations about living in the twenty-first century that lead us to examine ourselves in light of these reflections. Paperback, 208 pages (ISBN 1-888212-27-6) Order No. 005132—$13.95*

Thirsting for God in a Land of Shallow Wells
by Matthew Gallatin

Beginning in the street ministry days of the Jesus Movement, Matthew Gallatin devoted more than twenty years to Evangelical Christian ministry. Nevertheless, he eventually accepted a painful reality: no matter how hard he tried, he was never able to experience the God whom he longed to know.

In a moving narration, Professor Gallatin reveals why he became Orthodox, and explains the theological differences between East and West with grace and thoughtfulness. Paperback, 192 pages (ISBN 1-888212-28-4) Order No. 005216—$14.95*

Our Hearts' True Home
edited by Virginia Nieuwsma

Our Hearts' True Home presents fourteen warm, inspiring stories of women coming into the Orthodox Faith. These women come from a wide variety of backgrounds, yet there's a common thread: no matter how they struggled, their journeys are infused with the love and mercy of God. Paperback, 178 pages (ISBN 1-888212-02-0) Order No. 002109—$12.95*

Becoming Orthodox: A Journey to the Ancient Christian Faith
by Fr. Peter E. Gillquist

The inspiring story of over two thousand evangelical Christians and their search for historic Christianity. This book is for evangelical Christians on their own search for the Church and for Orthodox Christians looking for renewal. Paperback, 191 pages (ISBN 0-9622713-3-0) Order No. 000049—$13.95*

Christ in the Psalms
by Fr. Patrick Henry Reardon

How can we perceive the image of Christ shining the the Psalms? *Christ in the Psalms* is a highly inspirational book of meditations on the Psalms by one of the most insightful and challenging Orthodox writers of our day. Avoiding both syrupy sentimentality and arid scholasticism, *Christ in the Psalms* takes the reader on a thought-provoking and enlightening pilgrimage through this beloved "Prayer Book" of the Church. Paperback, 328 pages (ISBN 1-888212-20-9) Order No. 004927—$17.95*

Gender: Men, Women, Sex, and Feminism
by Frederica Mathewes-Green (Selected Writings, volume 1)

Frederica Mathewes-Green is a popular speaker and author, a commentator on NPR's "Morning Edition" and a columnist for Beliefnet.com. This series provides a selection of Frederica's best writings on contemporary issues relating to Gender, Culture, Ethics, and Faith. Her original and thoughtful insights are expressed in a style that is fresh, personal, and frequently humorous. She examines modern-day challenges from a perspective of ancient wisdom, as one who seeks to be deeply grounded in the faith of the early Christian Church. Paperback, 196 pages (ISBN 1-888212-31-4) Order No. 005660—$15.95*

---

*Note: prices listed were current as of September, 2002. Prices are subject to change. Prices do not include tax or postage & handling charges. To request a Conciliar Press catalog of other books about the Orthodox Faith and Church life, to place a credit card order, or to obtain current ordering information, please call Conciliar Press at (800) 967-7377 or (831) 336-5118, or log on to our website: www.conciliarpress.com